"This is a positive book from start to finish. The authors write clearly and crisply. Readers can open to the chapter that most speaks to them and gain advice on immediate action steps in a wide array of work-life issues. Jim and Linda know what they're talking about. They not only tap right into accurate feelings of this generation, but they lay out strategies for pursuing renewed careers. They use examples, case studies, research, provocative quotes, references, and their own experience to remind us that there are many pathways to staying relevant in our careers."

—**Beverly Kaye**, founder/CEO of Career Systems International;
coauthor, *Love 'Em or Lose 'Em: Getting Good People to Stay*;
author, *Up Is Not the Only Way*

"*Work Wanted* is a well-organized, useful resource for informing and encouraging all adults, not just boomers, as they plan for and live through their encore work years."

—**Jean E. Jordan**, Ph.D., social gerontologist

"This book should be a 'must read' for boomers anticipating retirement. Not only will it ensure a smooth transition, but it will be instrumental in reducing anxiety and fear about this most important life change.
This is great content for a retirement planning seminar. Statistical information, coupled with the anecdotal highlights, makes for interesting reading. Add the step-by-step discussion of what to do and how to do it, and you have workshop material that would have attendees leaving with a solid plan."

—**Lorraine Ballato**, gardening writer and former corporate executive

"This is an important book for baby boomers and the companies that employ them. Great ideas and different ways to look at things. Speaking as a baby boomer, I received numerous ideas for how to make the next stage of my life as exciting as previous stages. As a human resources professional at a Fortune 500 company, I learned of opportunities and challenges our company will face as the baby boomer generation reaches traditional retirement age."

—**Joann M. Eisenhart**, Ph.D., Vice President,
Human Resources, Pfizer Inc.

"Drs. Walker and Lewis offer a comprehensive resource for both boomers and talent management professionals. Pragmatic tools and advice equip boomers to make sound career decisions to craft a meaningful, productive professional life well past their 60s. Well-grounded in research and the realities of today's business environment, the book debunks prevalent age bias that inhibits organizations from hiring, engaging, and retaining talent that bring a wellspring of knowledge, experience, and wisdom."

—**Bill Huffaker**, Global Talent Management,
Visa Inc.

"For those of us who enjoy being active, both professionally and personally, the book delivers insight and details alternatives to consider in the next phase of our lives. This is an inspiring book for baby boomers contemplating retirement. This book provides insight to choices and alternatives rather than discussing traditional retirement planning."

—**Vera Teller**, Ph.D., Director of Systems and Programming,
Trader Joe's Companies

"*Work Wanted* brings tough love to the party by peppering us with questions and dilemmas we would prefer to ignore. It's a great new resource to those making a transition. For people who are acutely aware of the importance of reconciling dreams with means, having a clear sense of purpose and being rooted in the attainable, it's all about asking difficult questions, being honest with oneself, and being bold. *Work Wanted* is a great new resource to those now making the transition."

—**John Lavelle**, former senior strategy advisor,
The World Bank

"This is an important resource for those who want to keep working, want to work differently, or want to stop working and venture into new areas. There are many different ways to retire—none of them right or wrong—but all worth thinking about before leaving your current position. The authors address these issues in a nonjudgmental manner, helping readers to make a smooth transition while maintaining a sense of worth and purpose. I wish it had been available to help me with my own choices."

—**Harriet Landau**, Ph.D., attorney and executive coach

"*Work Wanted* is a great guide for 'later-in-life.'"

—**Sandra Parks**, assistant professor, Career and Technical Education,
Murray State University

WORK WANTED

WORK WANTED

PROTECT YOUR RETIREMENT PLANS IN UNCERTAIN TIMES

James W. Walker
Linda H. Lewis

Vice President, Publisher: Tim Moore
Associate Publisher and Director of Marketing: Amy Neidlinger
Wharton Editor: Steve Kobrin
Acquisitions Editor: Jennifer Simon
Editorial Assistant: Myesha Graham
Development Editor: Russ Hall
Operations Manager: Gina Kanouse
Digital Marketing Manager: Julie Phifer
Publicity Manager: Laura Czaja
Assistant Marketing Manager: Megan Colvin
Cover Designer: Alan Clements
Managing Editor: Kristy Hart
Project Editor: Anne Goebel
Copy Editor: Paula Lowell
Proofreader: Water Crest Publishing, Inc.
Indexer: Lisa Stumpf
Compositor: Jake McFarland
Manufacturing Buyer: Dan Uhrig

© 2009 by Pearson Education, Inc.

Publishing as Wharton School Publishing

Upper Saddle River, New Jersey 07458

Wharton School Publishing offers excellent discounts on this book when ordered in quantity for bulk purchases or special sales. For more information, please contact U.S. Corporate and Government Sales, 1-800-382-3419, corpsales@pearsontechgroup.com. For sales outside the U.S., please contact International Sales at international@pearson.com.

Company and product names mentioned herein are the trademarks or registered trademarks of their respective owners.

Printed in the United States of America

First Printing February 2009

ISBN-10: 0-13-235464-0

ISBN-13: 978-0-13-235464-6

Pearson Education LTD.

Pearson Education Australia PTY, Limited.

Pearson Education Singapore, Pte. Ltd.

Pearson Education North Asia, Ltd.

Pearson Education Canada, Ltd.

Pearson Educatión de Mexico, S.A. de C.V.

Pearson Education—Japan

Pearson Education Malaysia, Pte. Ltd.

Library of Congress Cataloging-in-Publication Data

Walker, James W., 1941-
  Work wanted : protect your retirement plans in uncertain times / James W. Walker, Linda H. Lewis.
    p. cm.
  ISBN 0-13-235464-0 (hbk. : alk. paper)
  1. Retirees—Employment. 2. Older people—Employment. I. Lewis, Linda H. II. Title.
  HD6279.W35 2009
  331.3'98—dc22
                          2008023259

Contents

About the Authors

James W. Walker, Ph.D. is a consultant, speaker, and author on human resource strategy and contemporary workforce management issues. Jim led The Walker Group, a consulting firm, for 20 years. Previously, he was with Towers Perrin for 15 years, where he was a vice president and practice leader, based in New York.

He was author of the award-winning textbook, *Human Resource Planning* (McGraw-Hill College), regarded as seminal in the field. He was an author or editor of nine other books and many professional articles, mostly relating to this subject. He was founder of the Human Resource Planning Society and has been active in many professional activities.

Jim has long had an interest in the field of aging and work, having led research projects on retirement while at Towers Perrin and having written and consulted on the subject. He and his wife, Harriet Lazer, co-authored a book, *The End of Mandatory Retirement: Implications for Management* (Wiley), which was also published in Japanese.

He earned a B.S. from Millikin University, and an M.A. in labor and management and a Ph.D. in business administration from the University of Iowa. Upon graduation, Jim was an assistant professor of management at Indiana University and San Diego State University. Later, he was an associate professor of management at Arizona State University. For contact information, visit www.walkergroup.com.

Linda H. Lewis, Ed.D. is a consultant, organizational development practitioner, and university professor with experience in both the public and private sectors. Whether teaching graduate students during her 10-year tenure at the University of Connecticut or mentoring doctoral students at Fielding Graduate University, she is a long-standing champion of adult learning and development. As senior vice president of Learning & Education at Charles Schwab & Co., Inc., VP of Strategic Change & Human Resources at Kaiser Permanente, and VP of Corporate Education for The Travelers Companies, people development has always been a priority for Linda. When running corporate universities, leading major change initiatives, or guiding dissertation research, her passion for lifelong learning informs her practice.

Linda earned a B.A. from U.C. Berkeley and UCLA, an M.S. in management and administration from Pepperdine University, and a doctorate in adult learning and adult education from Oregon State University. She serves on several non-profit boards and maintains a long-standing commitment to workforce development and managerial leadership.

Preface

We have had satisfying careers in university teaching, consulting, and working with corporations. In recent years, we have had no intention of slowing down, dropping out, or retiring. We weren't likely to start new careers. However, we wanted to find new ways to continue to do meaningful work based on our strengths.

When our professional colleagues and friends expressed the same view, we questioned why professionals should feel they are expected to retire, particularly when employers need the critical skills that they have. We questioned why they would scale back their lifestyles instead of continuing to work, earn, and save. We questioned why boomers, who have influenced our culture in every decade, would not redefine retirement and work to meet their own goals. Boomers should, we argued, dispel the long-held myths that define aging, work, and retirement.

So we wrote this book. It felt good. We learned a lot. And we now know that instead of retiring in the traditional sense, we will simply be "moving on" and "doing different things." We encourage you to do the same.

Because of our academic and consulting backgrounds, we've given you more than a simple guidebook. We've distilled the relevant research and facts to guide your choices of work, leisure, learning, and community or family activities. Our choice of publisher, a respected business school, reflects our emphasis on issues, challenges, and decision-making.

We thank Wharton, Fielding Graduate University, and all of our colleagues, friends, and family who influenced our work and share our conviction that as a boomer you can again "do your own thing."

—*Jim Walker and Linda Lewis*

Introduction

Old Myths, New Realities

As a baby boomer, born between 1946 and 1964, you are likely to think differently about your future than did past generations. You are poised to enjoy a healthy active life for two or three decades after age 50 and live well into your 80s or 90s. You can look forward to many active years and a variety of unprecedented opportunities and choices for work and leisure.

You will likely want to make your own choices. This requires you to challenge attitudes and practices among employers and in society that do not serve you well. As a boomer in a managerial, professional, or technical occupation, you have strengths, capabilities, and opportunities that you can leverage to advantage. Even though you may have the income to "drop out" and play golf, travel, or simply retire, you may instead want to continue your lifestyle, continue to earn income, grow your retirement assets, and sustain your fitness in order to work and enjoy other activities. You may continue working, gradually phase into retirement, switch to another company or different type of work, go back to college, or become a free agent professional (consultant, contractor, volunteer, or entrepreneur).

Everyone has his or her own situations and stories to tell. Bruce and Carolyn reflect circumstances that many boomers share:

> Bruce is thinking about his future plans but has near-term priorities. He and his wife, Carolyn, have three children. He has been an electronics engineer with a high-tech company for 20 years and at age 55 is a highly respected expert at the top of the company's technical career ladder. However, his salary is topped out and he expects only modest increases from here on. His annual bonuses have dropped because his division's profits are not

growing as fast as other divisions. He has thought about retiring, but the company has reduced its pension and retirement health care benefits. He has accumulated about $1 million in the savings plan (401k), but has recently seen the balances decline as the stock market has wavered. It is difficult to put away more money into savings. Carolyn has been working part time as a book keeper for a local medical practice.

They have a daughter about to go to college, an older daughter attending fashion design school, and a son who recently left the Army. All three are living at home and relying on their parents for support. Mark, at age 23, returned from service in Iraq a year ago. He has found it difficult to find and keep jobs or to take college courses because of the adverse effects of prescription drugs he must take to alleviate pain resulting from injuries received. Bruce isn't sure what their futures hold, but he knows that he's being counted on for encouragement and financial support.

Bruce enjoys his work, and especially the challenge of staying abreast of new technical advances that may enhance the company's products. He is old enough to be looking ahead to retirement, but is expecting to stay at work in his current job, as long as he can. He was invited to join several colleagues in forming an independent engineering consulting business, but felt the financial risk was too great. He enjoys hiking and fishing in the nearby mountains with friends and maintaining his classic Ford "woodie" wagon. With his family, he devotes considerable time in church-related activities. "In five years or so, I'd like to make some changes. Carolyn and I want time to do new things together. I'll probably keep working, but maybe part time in a smaller business. In the meantime, we're both going to keep working and help our kids get out on their own."

The Boomer Generation

Boomers feel responsible for shaping their futures. Overall, boomers have been forceful in shaping their destiny in the past and are likely to shape the nature of work and retirement to meet their new goals. Accordingly, you will not be alone in pursuing opportunities to continue working, learning, and growing. In the next twenty years, boomers will swell the ranks of older workers as well as retirees. Many will blend work and leisure to find the desired personal balance. With the pressure from boomers, combined with the demand for managerial, professional, and technical skills, employers will learn to attract and retain older talent. This will become the norm, not the exception. The landscape will change.

Over the decades, boomers have been described as having unique characteristics as a generation. They are known to

- Work hard to get ahead and to feel needed and valued.
- Pursue work that is meaningful and that makes a difference.
- Value relationships at work, teamwork, and participatory leadership.
- Pursue self development and learning.
- Contribute time and money to nonprofit causes, often champion causes.

As they grow older, these characteristics are expected to lead boomers to return to school, pursue new jobs or even new careers, start businesses, and be engaged in nonprofit endeavors. Boomers are not likely to sit idly by. They will pursue new, meaningful activities.

Within the generation, which has been defined (somewhat arbitrarily) as spanning 19 years, there are important distinctions. The first wave of the generation, persons born between 1946 and 1955, had different experiences and thus different attitudes and expectations than the second wave of the boomers, persons born from 1955–1964. Because the conditions in American society changed during these times, the experiences of boomers influenced their concerns, aspirations, and how they faced choices.

Early boomers experienced the space race, the death of two Kennedys, race riots, and the rise of rock and roll (including the Beatles and Woodstock), and parents who followed the guidance of Dr. Spock. Although many of these boomers were the cusp of the generation and followed the paths and attitudes of their parents (the silent generation), a great many actively changed the face of American culture, as discussed in Chapter 8, "Engage Younger Generations." As teenagers through the sixties, they protested the Vietnam war, experimented with new lifestyles, and set new patterns for conspicuous consumption. As adults, they have worked hard to achieve career and financial success. Women entered the workforce in growing numbers and many pursued professional and managerial careers. Today these boomers are considering their opportunities to retire, to work, to start a new career, or create a portfolio of roles. Their children are typically on their own or in transition. They are considering pursuing unfulfilled interests in careers, travel, leisure, hobbies, or community service that are important to them.

Second-wave boomers were typically less proactive and more content to be observers of changes around them. They did not know John F. Kennedy, and instead grew up in the seventies in the tumultuous decade with Nixon, Ford, and Carter as presidents. They challenged the authority of institutions, including businesses and government. They railed at the consumption behaviors of older boomers whom they considered excessive. They gave more attention to their families—parenting and engaging with their children and pursuing work-life balance. Today most are in the peak of their earning careers and years away from making significant choices about work and retirement. Younger boomers will also likely be greatly influenced by the state of the economy during the decade ahead—affecting their work opportunities, their income and savings, and the circumstances affecting their families. They face greater uncertainties than the first wave boomers.

About This Book

This book will help you consider your opportunities and formulate plans for your active years ahead. We present eight persistent myths about aging, work, and retirement and their implications for you as a boomer. We encourage you to challenge outmoded notions of aging and retirement and determine your own vision and plan for your future. New realities, such as changing attitudes toward aging and retirement and emerging talent shortages, are opening up new opportunities for work and for transforming retirement into a blend of work and other meaningful activities. Our discussion will help you explore and reflect on the choices available to you and to think creatively about your future.

There is a large and growing body of research and data on aging and adult development, workforce issues, age bias, work, and careers that is not discussed in most retirement and life-planning books. This book is fact-based, drawing on this body of research. Further, we provide references to the information upon which we have relied to enable you to consider the facts and to draw your own conclusions. You can draw upon research studies, others' experiences, interpretations of boomers' unique characteristics, and emerging practices and trends reported in news, business, and social science publications to inform your decision-making.

Challenging Myths

You may have read warnings of a coming workforce crisis—a shortfall of talent resulting from the mass retirement of baby boomers, particularly gaps in managerial, professional, and technical occupations. At the same time, you and many other boomers may feel that you enjoy working, like earning money (and spending it), and are not likely to retire any time soon. Current attitudes and trends indicate that boomer professionals are very likely to reject traditional retirement and instead stay in the workforce for a few more years than usual, thereby helping to avert a critical talent shortage. Work opportunities, boomer capabilities, health and longer lives, and the distinctive motivations of boomers to earn, spend, and find meaning in life all are converging to redefine the options open to individuals as they approach age 55, 60, or 65. Boomers are challenging old myths about aging, work, and retirement and are embracing and creating new realities. In order to make enlightened choices, you will need to understand the landscape.

In a meeting with a group of human resource managers from a variety of large employers (more than half of whom were baby boomers themselves) to discuss work and retirement trends, we found most firmly believed that there will be a talent crisis. They thought that their companies will be scrambling to recruit, develop, and retain needed talent. Most noticeable was the fact that aging boomers don't figure into their analysis or planning for the future. In their view, boomers will continue to retire when they become eligible for retirement benefits, as did their predecessors. Boomers, they feel, will have ample retirement income to do the things they want. Even under voluntary staff reduction programs, retirees have left willingly and, seemingly, happily. They believe this even though the facts show that many people have not accumulated pension benefits as their careers progressed through multiple companies. They also fail to recognize that boomers have been poor savers, accumulating few assets other than their homes. Yesterday's retirees had different situations and expectations than potential retirees in the boomer generation.

These managers said that their companies would prefer to fill the gaps and vacancies with younger talent. Aging boomers, they said, work at a slower pace, resist change, and are averse to new ideas; many are, in their estimation, technophobic. From their perspectives, it is appropriate to offer training and developmental experiences to younger professionals. Boomers are blocking advancement for these individuals—forming a "gray ceiling"—and this obstructs succession planning and development of future talent. It was apparent that their companies had few professionals or managers over age 55—and would clearly not want to have any around who are in their 70s.

Will boomers change these employer attitudes? Will boomers demand work opportunities after age 60, rather than going quietly into retirement? Will they push back the boundaries that constrain choices today? Are they likely to make work places more hospitable to older workers or, better yet, to diminish the relevance of age as a consideration? It is too early to see clear evidence of change. The first boomers turned age 60 in 2006; the first applied for social security benefits in 2008. There are just too few boomers over age 60 in the workforce to make a visible difference. Major changes by the generation have not yet taken hold. In fact, some of the first-wave boomers, at the cusp of the generation, share values in common with the previous generation—and are covered by traditional pensions and health care benefits. However, by 2012 or 2015, when about half of the generation has crossed the 60 line, companies are likely to have responded and adapted to the pressures for change. By the time the full generation has turned 60 in 2024, the workforce will likely be far more balanced by age categories, just as the workforce became balanced by gender. Demography will be destiny.

In the meantime, what's a boomer to do? Stay young? Appear to be young? Marketers of age-defying pharmaceutical and cosmetics, cosmetic surgery, fitness programs, and diets (and supplements) target boomers who are trying to preserve youthfulness. But this merely reinforces a youth culture, sustains denial of healthy aging, and perpetuates a fear of growing older. When you are healthy, fit, and active through your sixties and seventies, chronological age doesn't matter so much. Boomers need to challenge the myths of aging and recognize that important capabilities do not decline. Indeed, the facts about aging are great news.

Sixty is not the new forty. It's the new sixty. I'm sixty. That's the way it is. Get used to it.

—Gail Sheehy

Myth: It's Too Late to Make Big Changes

Kathy Bates' character in the movie, *Fried Green Tomatoes*, aptly characterized the baby boom generation by saying, "I'm too old to be young and too young to be old." Having shaped trends in every phase of their lives, boomers are disregarding traditional views of aging and are redefining work and retirement. Boomers, born between 1946 and 1964, are not about to leave the workforce and retire quietly as their parents did. Instead, they will do everything they can to stay young—defying aging and decline, staying active in work and other pursuits, enjoying their lifestyles, and developing new ideas and capabilities.

In particular, boomers in professional, managerial, and technical occupations in the American workforce, now approximately 19 million strong, have the capabilities and the will to consider new alternatives for work and retirement. Fortuitously, the economy needs to retain boomers' experience and skills, lest there be a workforce crisis due to talent shortages. Many state governments are working to attract older boomers into government jobs. For example, California, where the 60-plus population will almost double to 8.7 million by 2020, expects to entice older boomer professionals to fill many of the 33,000 new math and science teaching jobs during this period.

The creativity, initiative, and strong will of the baby boom generation should not be underestimated. As teens, boomers molded their own identity as a peer group, ignoring or challenging not only their parents, but also the authority of anyone over 30. When they turned 30, however, being over 30 didn't seem so old anymore. In a similar manner, we can expect that boomers will once again redefine norms as their generation progresses into their 50s, 60s, and 70s as they are already doing. For many boomers like yourself, these may be the best decades of your life!

As boomers mature, new realities are emerging that provide conditions favorable for more varied and innovative career and retirement patterns than those of previous generations. For example, because of their improved health and longer life expectancy, age is not a useful marker of capabilities, vitality, or life interests. There is no roadmap with age markers. Chronological age will no longer be the driver of work and retirement decisions as it was in the past. Boomers will demand that their interests and capabilities be recognized and accommodated, just as they have throughout their careers.

Myth: Retirement Is a Cliff We Must Jump Off at a Certain Age

In the past, retirement meant total withdrawal from work and was characterized by an abrupt shift to a life of leisure and an eagerness to leave work rituals and responsibilities behind. Retirement for most people has meant the opportunity to spend more time on the activities they enjoy most. Traditionally, this implied travel, leisure activities, hobbies, and other community and social pursuits. An image of retirement communities, amiable senior social networks, group excursions, golf and bridge games, and sun-belt living was popularized by retirees who could afford a leisure lifestyle and enjoy it in good health. However, many retirees have reported that they would have liked to continue working for a few more years if permitted to do so.

In America, people have been expected to retire when they "get old." Among men, while 90% between 20 and 54 are employed, only 68% between 55 and 64 are employed. Among women, 75% between 20 and 54 are employed, but only 55% between 55 and 64. Employment drops off sharply for both men and women after age 64. The average retirement age today is 63 for men and 62 for women. At these ages, more than half of men or women are no longer participating in the workforce.

Boomers are challenging the traditional definition of work and creating in its place a myriad of more flexible work and retirement alternatives. Today, distinctions between work and retirement are blurring. Many boomers want to continue working, but in different ways. Some may gradually phase into retirement by working part-time, reinventing themselves, changing employers, starting a business, or pursuing new interests. A Merrill Lynch study indicated that 75% of boomers intend to keep working in retirement. They expect to retire from their current jobs at an average of 64 and then launch into a new career. Many want a different, more personally rewarding job. Others want to remain in the same type of work, but with more flexible scheduling. Self-employed workers, on the other hand, are the most likely to keep on working. Among the boomers surveyed, 42% want to cycle between work and leisure. Still other boomers may want to keep working, but at different things and a different place. They may want to leave the organizational life and schedules that they found to be all too comfortable and routine.

For many boomers, work continues to be the center of their lives. The workplace is where their obsessions lie, where their friends and social relationships reside, and where they gain satisfaction from accomplishment. For some, their preference is simply to continue to work in the job without retiring. Because mandatory retirement is illegal under federal law, there are employees as old as 80 or 90 working in companies countrywide (an exception has been airline pilots, currently restricted to age 65 for safety reasons). Notably, some employers promote continued employment of their older workers and consider it a competitive advantage.

Many workers retire and work in the same field with the same or different employer. Flexible options are of growing interest, including phased or gradual retirement, part-time work, or consulting and contract opportunities. Retirement may not mean withdrawal from the workplace, but instead merely the decision to begin receiving retirement benefits and then to work in different ways. Increasingly boomers are looking for new sources of satisfaction—ways to make their lives meaningful and significant. They are developing new mental models of what work means, envisioning new views of themselves and their identity, and rejecting the constraints of traditional career steps and hierarchical work environments.

Part-time or contingent work need not be considered less desirable than full-time work. In fact, surveys suggest that it is preferred by many. As companies seek greater workforce flexibility, both employers and employees are becoming more receptive. Employers are creating new options as boomers seek ways to extend their working careers. Because the marketplace balances supply and demand for talent by using part-time or contingent workers, as a boomer, you may accelerate this trend.

As more boomers near traditional retirement age, they will lead the way in tailoring jobs to their interests, skills, and expertise. In particular, professional and technical workers with critical market skills are negotiating with employers (or clients) about the terms and conditions of work, including the structure, scheduling, and employment relationship with the organization. Whereas Generation X and Y workers have advocated innovative policies and flexible work arrangements that allow greater work-life balance, aging boomers are embracing these options as well and are becoming vocal and demanding champions as well as users.

Myth: Boomers Can Afford to Retire

For decades, employer benefit programs provided attractive retirement income and health care plans to employees, particularly in larger organizations. Employees who were covered by a defined-benefit pension program could typically retire at age 65 with the expectation of a guaranteed retirement of 40% or more of their final-years' income. Many could retire early with a somewhat reduced annual income (with the pension reduction allowing for the additional years of income received). Additionally, retirees typically received health care benefits at little or no personal cost. However, these benefits are becoming significantly reduced or less common.

The proportion of the U.S. population covered by private defined-benefit plans has fallen from 40% to 20% in just the past two decades. In recent years, some defined benefit pensions covering large numbers of employees have been frozen or eliminated. In their place, or as supplements, are 401(k) or other employee contribution plans that accumulate savings and, typically, include company matching funds. Employer-provided health care benefits are also being cut back and personal coverage is becoming more expensive. These trends are expected to continue. Employers are cutting back, capping, or completely eliminating their retiree health benefits programs. Accordingly, health care benefits provided to retirees by employers will be significantly less generous than those current retirees receive today. Watson Wyatt estimated that the level of employer financial support will drop to less than 10% of total retiree medical expenses by 2031 under plan provisions already adopted by many employers.

As a result, it is a myth that boomers can count on retirement income as being sufficient to meet their needs. The new reality is that many boomers will continue to work as employees to retain health care benefits and to accumulate assets for retirement income. Boomer professionals who have limited accumulated savings or retirement benefits will likely need to earn income well into their sixties.

In recent decades, retirement programs encouraged early retirement. These defined-benefit programs allowed workers to retire before "normal" retirement dates, usually age 65. Although retirement income benefits received under early retirement options were reduced, early retirement options were attractive to a majority of those eligible. As more retirees took advantage of the offer, early retirement soon became a social norm and was "expected" by many employers. However, in recent decades, early retirement took a negative turn when it was used as a management tool to reduce staffing levels. For example, in 2006, half of all employees at Ford Motor opted to retire early under terms of a special buyout offer. Voluntary early retirement options, including special limited-time "window" provisions, became a gentler tool for "reductions in force" than layoffs or restructuring. As a consequence, early retirement is now perceived as forced retirement by many employees.

For many workers, early retirement is no longer an attractive financial proposition. Benefit income is proving insufficient, given longer life expectancy and rising living expenses and inflation. In many cases, early retirees have gone back to work after a few years to supplement their income. Elimination of guaranteed benefits under defined benefit pension plans and their replacement with defined contribution and saving plans has, in many instances, reduced the degree of income security available to retirees.

Compounding the situation is the fact that boomers have generally been poor personal savers. Gains seen in the dot.com era gave many hope of a substantial retirement nest egg, only to be disappointed and left with worthless stock options. Today, houses are the primary assets of many boomers, and values are vulnerable. As reflected in a 2006 MetLife study, 44% of boomers aged 55–59 are concerned about having enough money in retirement. Among the respondents, most had insufficient savings, and 18% expected to have no retirement income from pensions, 401(k) plans, or the like. More than 62% of these boomers indicated they wish they had done better financial and retirement planning.

Boomers are often motivated by lifestyle as a driver of financial need. They been known to spend freely (more so than their parents' generation) and to pursue lifestyle pleasures. For many boomers, income itself became an obsession, and many managers and boomer professionals enjoyed high levels of affluence. Today, at age 55 or 60, many boomers are still enjoying the "good life" and see no reason to stop working (earning) in order to live in the style to which they've become accustomed. Many still have big houses, second homes, and large mortgages. Further, some remain employed in order to provide substantial support to family members. And a significant number of boomers are supporting aging parents as well as adult children. An estimated 15 million boomers are providing substantial financial assistance and care for elderly parents. One boomer couple with whom we spoke travels to Florida regularly to check on aging parents they are supporting. Another recently "welcomed" back three adult children, along with their families, to live again "temporarily" in the family home when their loved ones were overcome with economic setbacks through divorce. Being caught in a three-generation "sandwich" drains boomer resources and limits their ability to plan for retirement.

Boomers question whether they will have enough income and health care coverage to carry them through 20 or 30 years of retirement. For these reasons, it is reasonable to expect that boomers will remain in the workforce well beyond the current retirement ages. Surveys indicate that upwards of three-fourths of boomers see themselves earning a paycheck in retirement. While many will need to find new sources of income, others will leverage their past experience to advantage, becoming independent contractors, starting their own businesses, or creating new employment relationships with their current employers.

It is noteworthy that financial institutions are seeking out older boomers to help them plan and prepare for retirement—a good idea, but a few years too late for many individuals. If a person continues working until age 70 rather than retiring earlier and drawing on retirement assets, the funds available would be 30% greater. Boomers understand this logic. The Merrill Lynch survey on retirement found that 54% say they will still be working after age 65. The study underscores boomers' desire to continue working for financial reasons and also to stay active, involved, and engaged at work.

Myth: Capabilities That Decline with Age Impede Work Performance

Getting older itself isn't a problem. It is true that some aspects of human vigor and capability peak in youth and decline thereafter. With age, most adults typically experience reduced mental functioning (especially cognitive and memory capacity), reduced physical activity (especially mobility and agility), and slower recovery from illnesses and injury. However, such capabilities diminish very gradually and at very different rates for different people. They are rarely impediments to productive work and other activities for persons under age 75.

Boomers are challenging the myths that the aging process will affect them in any limiting way, and with good reason. The new reality is that boomers are healthier than past generations and will be able to remain healthy and active longer. Most are focused on well being and healthy living and are working to age that way, striving to remain active and involved through their 70s and 80s. This goal is achievable, given medical advances, improved health care, and healthy lifestyles. Boomers retain the most relevant capabilities for day-to-day functioning well into their sixties and seventies. They strongly reject age alone as an indicator of their capabilities relevant to work roles. Particularly in professional, technical, and managerial roles, declines in capabilities may not be significant impediments to effective performance. They are, rather, reminders of aging that are unwelcome in youth-oriented cultures.

Baby boomer talent is typically as vital as younger talent and is a primary labor source in the coming decades. Employers need to look beyond chronological age and define the practical requirements for effective job performance. As more and more jobs require knowledge workers, limits related to doing physical work are becoming less important.

Many people believe that human aging may be halted or slowed through diet, calorie restriction, exercise, and living patterns. Boomers will do whatever they can to remain young, attractive, and active. The boomer generation is the beneficiary of truly life-extending medical treatments developed during their generation. Beyond life-enhancing benefits, boomers can take advantage of knee replacements, Botox, Viagra, and other innovations that improve the quality of life as they age. Contrary to myths of inevitable declines, individuals can influence their actions and continually make choices. Contemporary notions of aging present a dynamic, interdependent interaction of biology and self-determination. Boomers' new socially constructed world view is enabling them to transcend the boundaries of stereotypical thinking about aging. They are determined to "stay young" even as they grow older. Whether entirely serious or not, they have been heard to say, "I want to stay in shape until I die" or "I hope I die before I get old"—a line in The Who's 1965 hit, "My Generation."

When today's oldest boomers were born in 1946, their life expectancy was 66 years. Approximately 95% of these boomers are alive today, and now may expect to live beyond age 82. Note that life expectancy is an average—not a maximum. Indeed, a growing number of persons are living to 100 years of age. Various websites feature case studies and research on centenarians and super-centenarians that highlight how long and how well we can live. The interesting question to ask yourself is, "What would I do differently now if I knew I were going to live to 100?"

Lifestyle can have profound impacts and long-term benefits. Not smoking, remaining active every day, living with a sense of purpose, and being socially engaged all contribute to longevity. These are behaviors and attitudes that you can embrace and emulate. While having good genes is important, each day new knowledge and cutting-edge research emerges to inform and guide choices.

Gerontologists distinguish the "young old" (60–80) from the less-firm "old old" (80 and older). Boomers reject the label of being "old." Older, aging, senior, or even mature are adjectives that boomers dislike and rebel against. Words like elderly, geriatric, or senescent are reserved for the very old and infirmed. Most likely, boomers will coin new, more positive and hopeful language to describe their evolving state. Most importantly, boomers will not consider age alone as requiring them to retire. While the focus of baby boomers is on making the most of their "young old" years, you also need to plan ahead for your later years.

Myth: Boomers Continue to Work Primarily for the Money

While boomers' motivation to work may be to amass supplemental income, additional reasons drive many to continue work based on a desire for social interaction, satisfaction derived from making a valued contribution, and pleasure gained from belonging to a good organization. At 55 or 60, for individuals who want to stay connected and to continue contributing, it is not time to drop out. This is a highly productive period in the lives of boomer professionals whose work is less stressful and more interesting than it was in their early careers.

While some companies have developed reputations as employers favorable to older workers, many boomers want more than part-time employment in routine jobs. A Home Depot job or Wal-Mart greeter job is not what many have in mind. People want meaningful professional work that is fulfilling, motivating, or satisfying—work that they feel is important and significant. Boomers work not just for the money, but also for the stimulation, satisfaction, and opportunity to contribute, learn, and grow.

Some people began retirement with a brief period of exhilaration and liberation but later looked around for more meaningful activities. Some played all the golf they could for a year or more, or traveled to places they dreamed of, only to ask what they should do next. Many boomers retire and then return to work shortly thereafter. It may be continuing to do what they enjoy but in a different organization or as free agents. It may involve developing and performing work that builds on past experience and skills, but in a different area. It may include doing something different in the same organization—"creating a space." For many, meaningful work means activities that contribute to the greater good of the community or society—morally significant work.

Meaningful work is emerging as a strong and powerful trend in business and in the popular press. It is what drives innovation and productivity. It is also a defining characteristic of a "preferred employer" among all generations of workers. In order to retain talented, mature workers and tap the strengths of individuals who still have a great deal to offer, a business case can be made for the value that can accrue when employers and boomers partner to identify meaningful work. Doing so will not only enable boomers to contribute to organizations, but it will also enable them to simultaneously realize their personal goals.

Myth: Boomers Have Difficulty Learning and Changing

In American culture, the myth persists that learning and education are best left to the young. Young people are often perceived to be better able to learn, adapt, and change. Investing in the education of younger persons is seen as having greater and longer-term returns. These are assumptions that cannot stand the test of scrutiny, especially given all we know about adult learning and development. Boomers are challenging this bias because it influences individual choices and the opportunities available for personal growth.

The emphasis today is on current skills and knowledge, particularly with respect to rapidly evolving technology and markets. Employers prefer to invest in younger "digital natives" rather than retrain and redirect older workers who are "digital immigrants." Conversely, companies tend not to invest in retraining, development, or further education of older employees, instead focusing on maintaining performance in their roles. "Peaked and parked" is an insulting, outdated notion when it comes to baby boomers.

The emerging reality is that boomers are continuing their own personal growth and development. They are striving to stay current, competitive, and knowledgeable and therefore valued. They are taking advantage of new channels for learning, including adult education, self-directed learning models, distance education, and computer-based learning. They are rethinking careers and often going to "a new place," developing enhanced capabilities and expertise to undertake new and different kinds of work roles. And many are preparing for retirement by gathering knowledge, formulating plans, and making decisions about what paths they want to pursue actively.

Educators talk about "learning organizations" and our "learning society." Given the changing demographics of the population, there will be even greater emphasis on formal, informal, and self-directed lifelong learning. We will experience more age-integrated learning rather than age-segregated education. Adults and youths will sit side-by-side in college classes, as is often the case today, and this trend will continue. Learners of all ages in even greater numbers will access Internet-based learning resources and learn from this powerful medium. Even traditional "senior centers" are redefining themselves to welcome adults of all ages to participate in their educational programs and classes as merely adult or community centers.

Developing programs and learning opportunities for adults at all stages in their lives is a critical starting point for rethinking how to make development and training inclusive and available to adults of all ages. Many boomers did not take the time or have the opportunity to continue their education as their careers progressed. Today, they are eagerly buying books, taking courses, and otherwise pursuing personal growth. They are driving new approaches to continuing professional education and influencing college and university curricula.

Boomers are certainly interested in getting up to date on current technology, professional and occupational knowledge, and changes occurring in the world around them. However, they are also engaged in learning to pursue a new sense of purpose or refocus on new objectives and interests. They are often seeking better or different careers and personal improvement. Also, they are seeking social interaction and meeting social needs. In taking initiative for learning, they are being active, rather than passive, and hence taking charge of their lives as they grow older.

Past generations were guided through their careers in the context of career phases or life stages. The assumption was that age-specific periods in adults' lives determined age-appropriate behavior and activity. Although there are many variations of the framework, Gail Sheehy's categories are useful in that they suggest every person confronts a series of career transitions: entry (age 18–30), growth (age 30–45), mastery (45–65), and integrity (65–85). These patterns may apply to many boomers, but there will be many exceptions as the notion of age-appropriate behavior is challenged. In reality, careers are rarely so linear. For example, boomers who leave their jobs and start new careers as entrepreneurs in a different field are essentially cycling back to entry, growth, and mastery phases—with the intent of moving through them at an accelerated pace and thereby experiencing a wide variety of "mini-careers." Life stages are not fixed, and you have the opportunity to do what is best for you, without boundaries suggested by ages. You can call it your age of discovery, your "second middle age," or your pre-retirement years, as you desire.

You may want to extend your career, especially if you have critical skills, knowledge, or expertise. You may also want to try something different, requiring you to cycle back to focus on your personal growth—acquiring new knowledge and skills needed to stay abreast of changing demands and opportunities or to pursue a new field. You need not follow the life phases and career paths that others have followed. You can challenge the myths of aging, work, and retirement. You can push back the boundaries of custom and shape your own future.

Myth: Jobs Are Not Available for Boomers

Many books, articles, and speakers argue that there is an imminent crisis in the labor force. If boomers retire at the same early ages as workers did in the past two decades, the result will be a significant loss of vital knowledge and a shortage of critical talent for organizations.

Generation X, which follows the boomers, is a smaller talent group, and it will be years before Generation Y talent is ready to take on critical professional and managerial roles. The losses may be particularly severe in certain industries (for example, oil, gas, energy, and health care) that rely on specialized skills and expertise and in specific organizations where a great number of boomers perform in critical roles.

However, we believe this crisis is a myth. Demography is not destiny, and talent shortages have a way of being filled (nature abhors a vacuum). The interaction of supply and demand in a dynamic labor market will result in a self-correcting balance. Ironically, unfilled talent demands mean *more* opportunities for boomers to stay at work. If a substantial number of older boomers continue working in professional, technical, and managerial roles, the talent pool will be sufficient to bridge the gap to the younger talent supply. Gen X talent, long in the shadow of the boomers, will have opportunities to progress more rapidly as vacancies occur. High-potential Gen Y talent may have early opportunities to prove their mettle.

Boomers have the capacity to change the trends and past patterns of work and retirement. As they shift their mental model from being "older" to being "more experienced," they will reject organizational limitations on their careers. Believing the mantra of "building on your strengths" promoted by Marcus Buckingham and others, many boomers are pursuing options with optimism and vigor.

If boomers are recognized as potential workers instead of probable retirees, they will ease imbalances in the workforce. As noted, boomers have financial incentives to continue working past 65. Employers who offer work tailored to abilities and interests, stay-put bonuses, attractive contracts, flexible schedules, and telecommuting are likely to be successful in retaining boomer talent.

Even with fewer retirements, there are other factors that will minimize the potential for a serious talent gap. One is that the demand for workers is likely to lessen as a result of changes in how work is performed. Fewer workers are required because of increased productivity and technology applications. Corporations typically eliminate, combine, or otherwise redesign jobs and organizations in conjunction with the outflow of talent through turnover, staffing reductions, and retirements. Additionally, the trends of outsourcing and off-shoring of work results in elimination of jobs and typically involves redefinition of many remaining jobs. However, the increase in older workers and resultant loss of workers through retirement will be gradual—more of a glacier than a flood.

Myth: Boomers Must Compete with Younger Generations in the Workplace

In recent years, considerable attention has been given to the unique behavioral characteristics of younger generations in organizations. The intent is to help managers understand the motives, needs, and behaviors of young employees and prospective employees. But while focusing on younger generations and attracting and retaining high potential talent, many organizations have missed opportunities to build intergenerational understanding and teamwork. The myth is that Gen X and Gen Y, representing the future, should receive special attention, at the expense of boomers. Boomers are frequently considered to be radically different from younger generations, outmoded in a changing society, and are therefore undervalued.

There is no denying that generational differences exist. Generations are variations on the relationship between life experiences and group behavior. However, characteristics associated with different age groups often become stereotypes. We believe that viewing generational differences should be examined to facilitate awareness rather than serving as a simplistic way to paint generational cohorts with the same brush. Although differences among boomers and Gen X and Gen Y individuals may suggest incompatible world views, understanding the socio-historical factors that contributed to the values, behaviors, and work ethics of each can go a long way toward promoting intergenerational collaboration. Fewer miscommunications, less confusion, and fewer flash points exist as individuals from different generations interact and discover that collaboration and shared learning are beneficial.

Gaining a fuller appreciation of generational characteristics and sharing alternate perspectives with workplace colleagues is one way to bridge gaps. For example, while many boomers were socialized to see themselves as stars, tend to keep attention on themselves, and are workaholics who question linking fun with work and or learning, they are also optimistic individuals who value personal growth and development.

Slower to embrace new technologies and ideas than technology-savvy Gen Xers, boomers often struggle with new technologies and don't want to be embarrassed by their limited facility. As a result, ambitious, team-oriented boomers may not relate well—whether as managers or as parents—to technology-wise Gen Xers in the workplace who tend to be self-reliant, fun-loving, risk-taking, and skeptical. It seems only a few decades ago that boomers felt that their parents and managers did not relate well to them. Generation gaps have always existed, but they may have been—and continue to be—overdrawn. The perception of alienation is far greater than the reality.

Today many managers in organizations are boomers. It is to their credit that attention to next generations has been intensive. In order to achieve their goals, including extending their working careers, boomers will effectively leverage the talents of the younger generations. By capitalizing on the strengths of Gen Y individuals who want to keep work fun, fast, and interactive, boomers can optimize the strengths of this talented cohort by fostering playing by the rules and fostering teamwork. Boomers, as managers, are making the benefits of work long-lasting for their own sakes as well as for the next generation of talent. It will be boomers who shape and lead the transition to becoming 21st century organizations during the next 20 years. They can avoid generational conflict and instead find tremendous opportunity for collaboration.

Active boomers—working to make contributions, stay young, and remain vital—will redefine social norms, making possible the many opportunities discussed in this book. In so doing, they will ally with younger generational talent to create opportunities and set new benchmarks for career and work styles.

1

Boomers, Do Your Thing Again!

There are no rules for how we behave at forty-two or fifty-nine. We will decide what is right and appropriate for us. We will take chances; we will seek out or create jobs that fulfill us, volunteer work that sustains us, family and friends who nourish us. We are not marching through prepackaged decades, checking them off on some master life list.

—Susan Crandell, *Thinking About Tomorrow*

Myth: It's Too Late to Make Big Changes

Under a widely held view, you have three phases of life: education (and growing up), a career (working, raising family), and retirement (withdrawal to a life of leisure). This implies that your career is monolithic and when it is over, it is over. Your destiny is retirement. You cannot change course, nor can you put off inevitable decline and withdrawal in your senior years.

As the earlier quote suggests, it is never too late to change course—to take on new interests, skills, and activities, or even reinvent yourself. Most people need to redefine themselves at some point between age 35 and 70. You may even feel a need to do this multiple times during the long span of your adult years. You face your own unique set of challenges and will make your own unique choices. There is no single path; you need not follow the paths of others. In the years ahead, you will have ample opportunities to step up and seek out the options that are meaningful and appropriate for you.

Whereas the typical worker of the nineteenth century was a farmer who worked the earth until he or she died or became incapable, today's workers are primarily knowledge workers who need to adapt to new challenges and opportunities. You are likely to continue to work, but you will take on new and different working roles—whether for pay or not. It is likely that you may not retire until you are 70, 80, or older; if you stay active and adaptive, you may never fully retire.

As a boomer, you have the advantage of being a member of a self-reliant, independent, and sometimes rebellious generation. Active boomer professionals are working to stay fit and active, make contributions, and remain vital. In so doing, they are setting new standards and expectations regarding careers, work, and retirement—charting new paths for younger generations to follow. Most boomers have had multiple jobs (and often major career shifts), marriages and divorces, and relocations. As a result, boomers will make personal choice the norm, not following a lockstep pattern of life phases. The new realities of today's world provide opportunities for you to be active and healthy for decades more, to continue to enjoy life, and to prepare for a secure retirement, when and if you want this experience.

In this chapter, you consider how you can effectively make choices affecting your future as a boomer. First, you ask yourself questions that are essential to self-reflection and assessment by evaluating opportunities and making choices. These questions are similar to those you may have asked early in your career, but now need to be tailored to your experience and your more-fully developed sense of values and purpose. Next you consider the influence of your past choices and the influences of phases, cycles, or turning points in your life. You need not make choices based on your "phase in life," but you need to consider why you want to do what you want to do.

You have a variety of choices, ranging from minimal change in your life to radical transformation or reinvention. Exploring alternatives is useful when thinking about the scope and difficulty of choices you may make. This chapter also presents factors that may constrain or limit your choices among options, such as your financial situation, health, or family responsibilities. Constraints are important to consider, as you don't always have the freedom or the capacity to do what you wish. You will consider how to bring your thoughts together and turn them into a practical action plan, one that has specific, near-term steps that are aligned with your long-term direction.

Ask Yourself the Right Questions

For your choices about future work and retirement to be good ones, you need to assess the realities of your situation, consider your needs and goals, and evaluate your options. The following questions can help you make thoughtful decisions and lead you to your optimal choices:

- **Reality assessment**—What are your strengths and limitations? What are your critical capabilities? What is your financial picture? What are the assets on which you can rely?

- **Career accomplishments**—How can you leverage your experience? What are the specialty skill sets and competencies of which you are most proud? What professional and social networks can you tap to assist in your search to define your next steps?

- **Goals and aspirations**—What do you want to experience that you've missed so far in life? What interests you? What turns you on? If you had more time and resources, what would you most like to do? With whom do you want to spend your time? What do you want to accomplish? For what do you want to be known? What do you want your legacy to be? How do you hope to make a difference?

- **Opportunities and options**—What is your attitude about retirement? When is the right time for you to retire? What are the opportunities that are out there for you? What are the different options? What are their pros and cons? What are the obstacles that lie in your way? What is keeping you from achieving/accomplishing what you want? What risks are you willing to take?

- **Visioning**—How do you see your future? Among your circle of family and friends, who else shares your vision for the future? What would your life look like if the changes you envision were to occur? What will you gain? What would you lose? What do you want to be careful to avoid?

- **Action steps**—What life changes are you willing to make? What help or resources do you need to initiate change? What are your next steps? What is your timeline for action-taking?

In practice, making choices is often a step-by-step, evolutionary process. Decision-making is typically iterative as you jump from one choice point to another. Often we find ourselves taking action steps that make sense to us, but we aren't sure why or how to explain our decisions. Sometimes you may think you know exactly what would make you happy but then later find out life didn't turn out as you anticipated. When this occurs, you need to rethink your priorities and plans.

Often important life choices are serendipitous. We embrace opportunities as they arise, often without a lot of careful analysis or planning. For example, many of us got into our first jobs based on our college major (which was often not an entirely rational choice) or based on inputs from recruiters with whom we talked and offers we received. Opportunities to change jobs or companies are often responses to opportunities that arise or the result of initiatives taken by others recruiting *you*. At this time in your life, think about how you can be proactive—the initiator who identifies options and pursues opportunities.

Peter Drucker once said that strategy is not about future decisions, but about the future of today's decisions. Your good choices include consideration of both your immediate options and your longer-term future. You need to consider both the facts as you know them today—and also your expectations for the future. This is like a zoom lens. You focus close-up, but expand your lens to include wider considerations and changes that may possibly occur in the future that influence your decisions. Choices are decisions about actions you will take in the short-term, with consequences for the long-term. For example, you may decide at age 60 to start a business, but will you still want to be building it ten years in the future—working long hours and risking your retirement assets as investments in your endeavor? Alternatively, if you decide to retire early in order to travel to exotic places—a desire you and your spouse have long had—what are you likely to do in three or four years, after you have done "enough" traveling? If you expect to live twenty or thirty active years in the future, you are well advised to make today's choices with your future view in mind and be flexible enough to revisit your choices as the years go by.

> *When you climb a rock face you move up one small space at a time, sinking your grappling hook into a rock crevice just within your reach, pause to look around, and then move up and repeat the process. You climb the mountain, with a goal in mind, but it is an exploratory process, with each part of the climb within your immediate reach as you progress.*

—Rob Cahill

Reflect on Lessons Learned from Experience

At this stage in your life, with all the experience you have accumulated, you should be well prepared to consider your choices for future work and retirement. What are some of the lessons learned by others that you should consider? Here are a few.

Think Positively

Be very realistic about where you are, but very optimistic about where you can be. Consider the following:

- Engage your heart as well as your head. Unleash your imagination and stretch your potential. Follow your instincts—don't overanalyze. Go "straight from the gut" as CEO Jack Welch advised in his book of the same title. Or "think without thinking" as Malcolm Gladwell advised in his book, *Blink*. Relax and be yourself.
- Make your own clarion call—what excites you? What will be your ideal future?
- Ask yourself what value you will add in the future—what difference will you make to society, your organization, customers, or your family and friends?
- Recognize that just doing different things doesn't necessarily add up to changing yourself and your path for the future.

Changes need to be big enough to make a difference—letting go of the past and moving to a "new place."

Most people are optimistic when imagining how our own plans will turn out, believing ourselves to be more competent and in control than we actually are. And as we get older, we tend to recall our happy experiences more than the unpleasant ones. Research suggests that optimism is often self-fulfilling—your attitude helps you overcome adversity. At the same time, people tend to be more pessimistic about general, big-picture matters, such as global warming or world peace. As a rule, psychology looks at negative or discouraging factors rather than the positive ones. Martin Seligman, psychology professor at University of Pennsylvania, has argued that we should take the positive side of psychology and how people can build "authentic happiness."

Know Yourself

Always be authentic. Take the following into consideration when trying to find out your essence:

- Separate your past work role or job from the real (and future) you. Don't let your past jobs or roles define you for the future. Reach down into yourself and be the person you really are, and want to be.

- Face your self-limiting assumptions and attitudes and bring them up to your consciousness so you can deal with them. Were your past failures merely learning experiences? Have you avoided activities because you weren't sure you had the skills? Do you fear the unknown? Have you had a "can't do" attitude you need to overcome?

- Be honest about your personal progress and your satisfaction with it. You must be the judge of yourself and your work. Gandhi said, "Man becomes what he believes himself to be."

- Look for signs of real change and celebrate them. Don't let the illusion of change keep you from making substantive progress. Companies often restructure and implement cosmetic changes that conceal shortcomings that ultimately slow growth and development. Don't let this happen to you.

- Use self-assessment tools to identify your strengths and weaknesses, interests, and "drivers." Several books provide detailed checklists such as in the book by Sadler and Miners or websites such as authentichappiness.com, futuredecisions.com, or 2Young2Retire.com.

- Authenticity means being yourself—how you present yourself to others, how you interact with others, and what you are, are all consistent with your real personality and character. You are genuine if you are not "faking it," trying to kid yourself or others that what you are saying is consistent with your behaviors. Authenticity requires that you know yourself well, that you reflect the qualities you've had through your life, and that you adapt (but not too much) to social norms, so that you represent your inner self, and you aren't acting.

Don't Go It Alone

Don't depend solely on yourself; rely on input and support from your friends, family, and colleagues, as follows:

- Acknowledge that you are not alone in facing choices. Many others are grappling with similar issues and trying to figure out how to move forward in uncharted territory.
- You can also rely on professionals and consultants to assist you with fact-finding, analysis, and assessment of your unique situation.
- Develop a knowledge and awareness of issues that will spark discussion and dialogue at home and in the workplace, creating momentum and shining the spotlight on this topic.
- Learn from the experience of others and from common themes and lessons learned.

It is important that you at least talk with your spouse, partner, or significant others. A Fidelity Investments survey of 502 couples found that 41% of couples gave different answers when asked whether one spouse would work in retirement. Men often underestimated how long their wives would continue to work. When asked whether their nest egg would allow them to lead a comfortable existence, 37% of the couples gave different answers.

Bring Your Thoughts Together

Create your mental model of where you are and where you are going:

- See all the factors that affect your choices and your future. Too many poor decisions made about relocations or new jobs are based on thinking too narrowly and not considering the implications.

- Challenge your own thinking. There are no right or wrong answers—just those that are the best fit for you. Your answers build on one another—and become a completed puzzle. Over time, you will fit in all the pieces of your vision for the future.

- Understand the difficulties of doing what you want to do. Are opportunities open to you? How well prepared are you for your choice? Will working independently as a free agent professional be difficult for you? Are you prepared to adjust your living expenses to afford a low-income choice?

- Know the difference between hard facts, myths, and assumptions. Challenge information that you receive and verify that it is reliable. Often it is not necessary to go back and reassess basic personal values, vision, dreams, and passions. Boomers don't change much in terms of fundamentals, but merely return to them and bring them into sharper focus. There is an old saying that "As you grow older, you become even more like yourself."

- Practice your elevator speech. A concise, positive answer to the question, "What do you do?," represents your current life without boring or confusing other people. One author suggested that boomers may be involved in so many activities that it would take a half hour to explain. Don't go there. Keep your story brief, interesting, and to the point. When others ask, "How are you?," they are not asking for a full health report.

Chart Your Own Future

Be aggressive in pursuing the opportunities you desire. Try out these techniques:

- Make clear commitments to action. It is easier to talk about making changes than it is to behave differently. Set specific action plans, goals, and timing. Be businesslike.

- Have courageous conversations with others who have the power to open doors for you—even talking with those who may put up barriers or close doors (for example, because of age bias).

- Take risks to get out of your comfort zone and move to a new place, whether or not you or your world is ready.

- Decide what you will leave behind—the activities you will stop doing—in order to free up your mind, your assets, and your time to do new, future-oriented activities.

- Feel empowered to do what you really want to do and what you need in order to ensure a secure and satisfying future.

- Customize your choices and press your employer and others to accommodate them.

- Consider alternatives and afford yourself the luxury of experimenting with different options.

- Be prepared to suffer adversities and then bounce back. Athletes talk about recovering from losses and personal setbacks; you must do the same. For example, an empty-nest couple sold their home and moved into a small condominium in La Jolla village; however, six months later they decided they could not live in such cramped quarters. They sold and bought a larger home, demonstrating their resiliency.

If you feel stuck, step back and analyze why. What caused your crisis or impasse? What issues need to be resolved? What are the assumptions and your own patterns that keep you from taking positive action? Several books are available to help you move forward.

Life's Twists and Turns

Your choices are affected by your experiences in life, your joys and pains, and the concerns you feel. These are often attributed to phases or stages of your adult life:

- As a **youth**, you established your own identity and self-worth, separated from your parents, and gained independence.

- As a **young adult**, you completed your education, explored options, and ambitiously pursued a career; you became a self-reliant, contributing person.

- As an **adult**, you strived for significance at work and in your career; you built deep relationships with family and friends.

- As a **middle-aged adult**, you realize that some ambitions will not be met and you work through who you truly want to become, what is most meaningful to you, and what you want to achieve.

- As an **older adult**, you are more selective in your activities, aiming to enjoy life, sharing what you have learned and mastered; giving back to the community, and leaving a legacy for the next generation.

- As an **elderly adult**, you will value integrity and wisdom, seek social interaction to avoid loneliness, embrace healthy aging, and cope with issues. Ultimately, you may become dependent on others for your care.

Stages of life such as these may help you reflect on your experiences and think about your future psychological development. Similar questions have been put forth by philosophers, authors, and psychologists for centuries and are popular because they have common appeal across generations. Because people tend to have similar experiences at roughly the same times of their lives, you may find comfort in knowing that what concerns you is similar to concerns of others. By taking life stages into account, you can roughly assess the challenges you will most likely face and benefit from learning how others overcame them. During transitions from stage to stage, you may experience discomfort, questioning, reassessment, and rediscovery, followed by consolidation and stability until the next transition.

Greek philosophers, most notably Hippocrates and Plato, defined eight stages of life, which were aligned with the forms of the soul, eight seasons of the year, and the celestial spheres (moon and planets). More recently, psychologists Erik Erikson, Daniel Levinson, George Valliant, and author Gail Sheehy, among others, have contributed insights from their research to the thinking about life stages or phases and life planning. Gail Sheehy's books have provided the most popular interpretation as she is a cultural observer of people's lives and development.

While age periods are traditionally associated with life stages or phases, they are defined by authors; individuals' experiences can vary widely. Growth and development from infancy, childhood, adolescence, and young adulthood are typically more sequential than adult phases. Recent research studies have shown that people simply do not live in predictable life stages. Transitions are triggered by life experiences and personal development; they are not necessarily tied to certain ages. Thus, you may want to reconsider your identity, your aspirations, and what is most meaningful to you at any age. For example, considerable attention has been given to the mid-life transition at age 40–45, the so-called mid-life crisis, and a particularly difficult transition for many adults. However, this introspection and redirection may occur at any time in life, occur more than once, or never occur.

Accordingly, it makes more sense for you to consider the concerns you face when you experience them without regard to your age. Consider the influence of your past choices and the influences of experiences or turning points in your life. You need not make choices based on your age or sequential phase, but instead you need to consider why you want to do what you want to do. Maddy Dychtwald argues in her book, *Cycles*, that we should follow a more flexible, open-door approach to life's options

In an era when you can join AARP (American Association of Retired Persons) at age 50, it is not very clear when old age sets in. AARP is no longer merely about retirement or seniors, but rather is a nonprofit, nonpartisan membership organization for people over 50. The organization promises "the power to make it better." "It" is broadly defined as the perceived interests of the members.

Boomers will typically have more years to spend after their children grow up and leave home than they spent raising them. As a result, as the role of parent fades, it will be overtaken by other roles and activities. As the saying goes, "Life begins when the dog dies and the kids leave home."

For boomers, the expectation is that most will be able to extend their careers or pursue other work and interests through their sixties and well into their seventies. Many persons remain engaged well into their eighties. However, for most persons, it will be difficult for reasons of health, energy, motivation, or age discrimination to continue this level of activity into their late seventies and eighties. At some point, boomers know they will have to cope with limitations on activities.

Where does retirement fit in? It is a choice to withdraw from the workforce—entirely or partially. However, retirement has many different meanings primarily shaped by marketing influences from financial institutions, retirement communities, marketers of leisure goods, and services companies. As such, retirement is essentially a self-declared state—an abandonment of work (at least full-time career work) and commitment to alternative activities—leisure and community involvement.

The Myth of a Heroic Life

You may have thought of your life as a journey much like a hero's journey. You find role models in biographies and naturally compare phases of your life with those of the heroic others. In myths from history, the hero typically goes through several steps that correspond to common life phases:

- A call to adventure, which the hero has to accept or decline

- A road of trials, in which the hero succeeds or fails

- Achieving the goal, which often results in important self-knowledge

- A return to the ordinary world, where the hero again can succeed or fail

- Application of the self-knowledge to improve the world

Core elements of the mythic stories of Buddha, Moses, Christ, Osiris, and Prometheus follow the structure. One particular author, Joseph Campbell, was fascinated by the myth of a heroic path; his analysis of the heroic myth was used by George Lucas in conceiving the *Star Wars* movies.

An important implication of the myth is that when we reflect on our experience at some point in our lives, we gain insights and wisdom that we can apply as we tackle new challenges. The myth is all the more relevant today. As the extension of our working lives, it gives us decades of opportunity to perform again, including accomplishments for the benefit of our community and the world.

Determine How Much Change You Want

The following sections discuss the alternative choice you can make, ranging from a little change to a lot of change.

Stay the Course

Keep doing what you are doing until you can't stand it or are thrown off course. Stay with your current employer and hang on to your job as long as you are able or you can tolerate it. In employers that permit it, such as government organizations, many employees are working well beyond 65 because they enjoy the work and their retirement benefits are continuing to grow. If you are a successful entrepreneur and you are enjoying it and sustaining your income, why stop? University faculty often continue in their positions long after age 65, many into their seventies, because of the stimulation their work provides.

At age 60, Sylvester Stallone decided to make a sixth movie about Rocky Balboa, after a 16-year hiatus. Sly observed, "People were saying the parade had gone by, and who was I to try and bring it back again? I just felt that I've had a lot of regrets in the past 15 years, and I had to go back and rid myself of this regret." The film, written by, directed by, and starring Stallone, is about a washed-up champion who insists on a last, doomed chance at a younger man's game. This might be considered a metaphor for Stallone's declining career fortunes. Stallone saw it not as a comeback, however, but an opportunity to avoid obsolescence. "An artist dies twice, and the second death is the easiest one. The artistic death, the fact that you are no longer pertinent—or that you're deemed someone whose message or talent has run its course—is a very, very tough piece of information to swallow," said Stallone in a *New York Times* interview. "Every generation runs its course, and they are expected to step aside for the next generation," Mr. Stallone said. "My peers are going through it right now, and they feel they have much to contribute, but the opportunity is no longer there. They're considered obsolete, and it's just not true. This film is about how we still have something more to say."

Renew Your Work Passion

Build on your strengths. You may not need or want to "reinvent" yourself. Rather, find ways to reawaken your love of your work, what you enjoy, or what you do well. Push yourself to go to the next level— reach to a higher standard, or reinterpret what you are doing. Change your context (different company, different orchestra, different geography) if it will further your renewal. For example, Audrey, an administrator in a community college, sought to qualify for a job with greater management responsibilities, and she recognized the need to obtain advanced education credentials. She's taking the necessary coursework while continuing to work and build relationships at the school.

As another example, an actor, a concert pianist, and an art collector in the French movie, *Avenue Montaigne*, rediscover and deepen their love of their respective arts. They have devoted their lives to art, but question what kinds of lives they have gained and have lost their passion. They cross their paths at a café and are influenced by a young waitress who came to Paris to look for her own fame and fortune. The waitress, Jessica, prompts reflection and redirection in their lives through her conversations with them. Renewal lies within us and welcomes a chance to emerge.

Sometimes individuals go back to earlier callings. Hope, a professor for many years, splits her time between a home in the U.S. and a small house in Mexico. Now instead of receiving a paycheck, she tutors townspeople who want to learn English in exchange for assisting her with construction, gardening, and cooking. As an added bonus, those she teaches are helping Hope perfect her Spanish. She finds this newfound bartering system the perfect way to continue teaching others and to make a difference while also benefiting from others' expertise.

For example, after graduating with a degree in education, Bob taught elementary school in a Florida city. Many of the children were from poor families, suffering from health, family, and other difficulties. The pay was low, and the school circumstances were frustrating. When he noticed an advertisement for jobs at a parcel delivery company, he moved. He built a career there, progressing through the ranks. His current role as an operations training manager draws upon his 32 years experience and affords a degree of flexibility in work hours. Training activities are conducted 24/7. Bob is now turning 55, and is eligible for retirement. He can continue in his role for another eight years, earning his salary and also accruing an annual 2% increase in his pension benefit. On the other hand, he is thinking about returning to his preferred vocation, teaching. With his degree, he merely needs to take two courses and pass a certifying examination to become eligible to teach again. "If I'm going to do this, this is the time to do it—not eight years from now," he said. With a son in college and two sons recently graduated from college, he and his wife are "empty nesters."

Create a To-Do List

Do those things you have always wanted to do. Keep a list and set priorities. Add things as you think about them and as they become important to you. Move actions up if you wish you could do them sooner. Some folks want to play more golf (or learn golf), learn guitar, travel through the Canadian Maritimes, or become involved in a community or charitable initiative. Learn Italian and travel to use it. For example, Jim always was "on the road" as a management consultant. Slowing down the consulting pace allowed him to join the local Rotary Club. Sherry wanted to join her condo association board "when she got time." When she changed jobs that had flexible scheduling, she put her name on the ballot and is now leading the association's landscaping committee.

As another example, Jerry got married and joined the FBI after earning a business degree in marketing and a law degree. He served three years as a special agent in Norfolk and Detroit. He returned to his Illinois home and went into private law practice after a few years in the prosecutor's office. Ten years later he was appointed circuit judge. At age 60, he retired. "No, I did not go back into private practice. I retired! I enjoy playing a lot of golf in the summer and hunting in the fall. We travel in the winter and we visit our grandchildren. Our 'things to do' list is still long but getting shorter."

Go for One Big Thing

Get serious about your life's passion—the one ambitious thing you've always dreamed of doing and worry that you'll never do it. Make painting your serious work, instead of a pastime. Climb Mt. McKinley or Mt. Everest. Sail west and don't stop. Write the novel for which you've been collecting ideas since you left college. Stan and Bev visited North Carolina many times and decided finally to build a new home and life there. Jeri and Bill had worked for others in restaurant and catering businesses, and set out to open their own pizza/Italian "heaven." From day one, it has been the most popular spot in town.

Sandy suffered through TWA's reduction in pay, elimination of pension benefits, loss of stock value, and ultimately, acquisition by American. At her career peak, she was flying entirely international flights. With the downsizing and mergers, she accepted flight assignments within the U.S. and gradually reduced her workload. When Sandy officially retired from American after 35 years of service, she received a coveted lifetime travel pass. While still flying part time, she earned a nursing degree. She is now working at a local hospital, where she receives health care benefits for herself and her husband, Rick. She and Rick feel they are well situated for continuing to work in the future for another five to ten years.

Transform Yourself

Get on with becoming who you really want to be. If you missed a mid-life crisis back in your thirties or forties, this is the time to make a dramatic shift in your life's direction. Re-examine your interests, your abilities, your dreams, and aspirations. Define your real purpose in life and your vision of where or who you want to be. An airline pilot retired early (as they often do) and became a certified financial advisor—not an easy thing to do. A bus driver, who used to work as a technician in a factory that closed some years ago, was determined to become an Episcopal priest. Many folks have chosen to become realtors, although the recent market downturn has made such a successful transition more difficult.

Diane has taken on new and varied roles since retiring early from an insurance company where she was a senior executive. At age 57, she was not eager to move into a full-time job in another company.

After retiring, she served as an executive-in-residence at Boston College. Soon she was asked by a local historic preservation society to serve as the interim director (without pay). "It was a huge adjustment, but I loved it," she said. She found that the small staff had a passion, drive, and tenacity that called for team building and problem solving with few resources. The staff appreciated her experience and leadership. That projected completed, she turned to pursue personal passions: taking piano lessons, studying dance and yoga, helping a conservation organization fight beach erosion, and spending time with her husband. Within several months, after considering her preferred focus for the years ahead, she enrolled in a program to earn a master's degree in elder care and is looking forward to making a contribution in this field.

Factors to Consider in Making Choices

For most people, finding meaningful work is not so much an inner self trying to get out (revealing your psyche or soul), but simply making the most of circumstances and opportunities as they change. There are often serious constraints on your freedom and capacity to make choices. Circumstances change, in positive, fortuitous ways and also in potentially adverse, impeding ways. You may not be aware of the facts that will affect your future and therefore you need to adopt fresh thinking about your opportunities and constraints. The following are some factors that can affect your decision-making process.

Financial

It is often said that money doesn't matter as long as you have enough of it. Continuing to earn money is important for people seeking to cover living expenses and accumulate savings for retirement. However, the necessity of working for income can crowd out the time you may want to spend in other non-pay activities.

For many, continuing to earn money is meaningful in itself. In American society, being an income producer has long been a mark of productivity—a reflection of accomplishment, self worth, and identity. Income and wealth are also markers in social networks, often determining the social circles and activities in which you participate (that is, whether you can afford to go on a cruise). In this instance, money does matter.

However, for most boomer professionals, whether or not work is compensated is a secondary consideration. Income is not their critical need or objective. Professionals over age 50 are more likely to embrace work that is *not* for pay—whether community or charitable work or "meaningful" leisure activities. Of course, you can earn income for work in non-profit organizations, but the motive of service is typically as important as or more important than the income.

Sufficient income or wealth permits you to spend their time as you want. You can give your time and donate assets freely for charitable purposes—supporting the motives of legacy and moral or spiritual purpose.

Health

Unfortunately, many persons have physical conditions that constrain the options for work and other activities. As discussed in Chapter 4, "Stay Healthy and Active," some people have limitations on their capabilities due to injury, illness, disease, or aging. According to a Boomer Project Healthcare Survey, 30% of boomers say they've survived a major illness and 3% have changed their diet due to a medical condition. Some boomers are finding that they need to adapt their choices of leisure and fitness activities because of knee or other joint issues. Others find that the stress of extensive travel or full-time work is too much to bear. Are there factors that might limit your choice of activities?

Serious illness or injuries are often a wake-up call for some individuals. Disability and disease remind you how precious life really is. Charlotte, a young boomer, had a burst appendix and was hospitalized for a month as she recovered. Back in action, she saw her priorities differently. Former activities did not seem as meaningful or important as they once were, and she set new priorities, focusing on family and community. A similar reaction occurs among persons with chronic conditions such as heart disease, cancer, HIV/AIDS, or diabetes. You have to decide how you can make the most of your years ahead. Rachel Naomi Remen, a physician, professor of medicine, and therapist, in her book, *Kitchen Table Wisdom*, offers thought-provoking anecdotes of people's battles with chronic diseases, reminding us that the challenge isn't about dealing with illness but rather life!

Many boomers are discovering the merits of fitness and greater personal attention to diet and health care. For them, health is an opportunity and a meaningful area of activity. At 55, Harriet remains steadfast in going to the fitness club for a 90–120 minute workout every morning. It is a "top of the day" priority that she has maintained. The statement that there isn't time to exercise becomes no more than an excuse when you decide that maintaining your physical well being is at the top of your "to do" list.

Others' Preferences

If you are living alone, you may make your own choices regarding work. However, if you are married or live with a partner, you will surely want to take into consideration the interests of this significant other in your life. Work schedule, work location, and the demands of work may need to be tailored to provide time and flexibility for travel, to be with grandchildren, and to engage in other activities. More importantly, you and your life partner may have been focusing on different interests and activities or going in different paths and directions over the years. Although working after retiring from or leaving an employer may offer more flexibility, it may also provide you with new or different opportunities to work or play with family members and significant others. Your relationships may also change as you give and take to do different things together.

Caregiving Responsibilities

You may be caring for aging parents, or even grandparents. You may still have children at home, or as often occurs, supporting children who seem to rebound frequently and come home when transitioning to a new phase in their lives. You may have dependent children with dependent children. Many boomers are the sole caregivers for their young grandchildren. Overall, half of all grandparents alive today are members of the boomer generation, and this number will increase as boomers' kids become parents. Approximately 40% of boomers are grandparents.

The Boomer Project National Study asked boomers for self-descriptions of their status. The responses were as follows:

- Grandparent: 41%

- Caregiver: 28%

- Child at home: 27%

- Child in college: 20%

Caregiving responsibilities can be a barrier to pursuing meaningful work or leisure activities. If this situation arises for you, you may want to aggressively explore alternative care providers—assisted living, support for dependents in their own homes, or assistance that is explicitly transitional (only for a short time). One couple found that selling their large suburban home and moving to a small condominium simply precluded the options of children or others residing with them. On the other hand, some extended families find great joy and satisfaction in caring for their members, referring to it as a calling or vocation.

Access to Desired Opportunities

You may find it difficult to locate the kind of work or activity that appeals most to you. While you may have some ideal jobs or roles in mind, they may be hard to find. As discussed in this book, employers are often reluctant to hire older workers as employees and are particularly reluctant to provide the flexible schedules or work arrangements that you may desire.

You also may also find yourself competing with others for work, even for volunteer roles. To gain a senior role in a nonprofit, you may need to "earn your stripes" and work your way in gradually. For example, beginning as a docent in a museum, helping out with fund raising, or serving on a project committee may be an entry role, not exactly what you want to do, but a first step.

Another constraint is the availability of the opportunities you desire. Year-round golf is not available in the colder climates. Opera and many of the arts are not usually available in smaller communities far from urban centers. If you have passions for certain work or other activities, you may have to consider relocating. Numerous books are available that ask you to identify criteria that are important to you and then correlate your responses to "the best places to retire" in America or the world.

Your Independence and Flexibility

Are you comfortable working on your own, as a free agent, or do you prefer working in an organization with other people and a management structure?

Upon retirement or leaving an employer, some boomer professionals take a gap year, similar to the year some high school students take off before going to college. They shift into neutral and catch their breath. They play golf, they travel, and they relax. After a year or two, however, most get restless and realize they need to be doing something productive—for mental stimulation, for social interaction, or to earn some money. That's when they search in earnest for meaningful activities.

Most, however, have not given a great deal of thought as to what might interest them sufficiently to draw them back into work activities. Few have a sense of passion for a new direction. Rather, they test different alternatives—trying out different kinds of activities through projects of six months or a year. It is a slow transition toward being in charge of your own portfolio of activities, much like being in charge of a portfolio of investments. In the same vein of trying out alternatives, some people rent rather than buy a house to check out a community in which they may want to retire. Short-term commitments enable you to retain your flexibility and make different choices if initial decisions don't turn out as anticipated.

Managers are typically accustomed to a well-defined work pattern—a specific job, an office or place to go to and work, set hours, and a daily routine. Withdrawal from work is a difficult transition. Those who decide to return to the workplace rarely find opportunities with large companies that resemble the ones they once knew. Rather, individuals must adapt to the new patterns of working in a smaller company, in a nonprofit organization, or as a free agent (contractor, consultant, part-time). More often than not, people move into activities that are not like those in their career, although the work may tap their key skills and abilities.

A study by MetLife showed that nearly one-third of persons over age 55 already are self-employed or owners of their own businesses. The current sectors and employers of older persons who work were as follows:

- Self-employed or owner: 32%

- Private sector businesses: 29%

- Education: 13%

- Government: 12%

- Nonprofit: 7%

- Health care: 4%

- No response: 3%

As boomers leave or retire from large companies, they are more likely to have the flexibility to adopt a portfolio approach for their activities. As a boomer, you are more likely to pursue work as free agents than to pursue full-time jobs with employers. Companies are expected to be more open to part-time roles or gradual retirement, as discussed in the Introduction of this book. Free agency gives you greater flexibility in implementing a portfolio life. You have the independence to make choices, assert your will, and not be confined by decisions of others.

John's Story: Why Retire at 55?

When I came to the bank 17 years ago, I felt it would be my last employer and that I would leave by age 55. I came to the bank because I outgrew my previous job and organization, and I wanted the larger responsibilities—and significantly higher pay.

I could have stayed at the bank until age 62 with zero risk of losing employment, and there would always be work for me to do. I'm in a pension plan that will give me a substantial monthly benefit at age 55. But if I were to stay, I could accumulate additional credits until 62 and the benefit would be based on the final three years' average pay. After the first few years, I felt I might stay on to maximize the benefits. I also felt my career was moving ahead—with work that propelled me to be curious, vibrant, and cutting edge. I stayed engrossed and engaged in bigger jobs.

Many of the people I worked with and relied upon have left the bank. My own work is beginning to seem repetitive and not as challenging as it once was. I could have rebuilt my network of bank contacts and stayed on. But I felt this would be like starting over and I've done this too many times. It seemed to be a good time to move on to new things. I know I am leaving a good organization and I have nothing against it. I'm leaving the security of the bank and a higher pension in order to do interesting work elsewhere and perhaps earn even more income.

I am good at analyzing situations, thinking systematically, and offering solutions. I help make sense out of messy problems. I have found that others appreciate the value of my help. Accordingly, I thought I would pursue interesting consulting work—and enjoying my new freedom and testing different alternatives. I am particularly intrigued with projects in China and eastern Asia. These opportunities will be more interesting than the ones here in the bank.

John's story is not dissimilar to that of other boomers who have gotten in touch with their strengths and desires and are capitalizing on their potential. Hopeful about the future and optimistic that good things are yet to come, John epitomizes the "can do" attitude of boomers. We encourage you to consider the many paths available to you and to be proactive in pursuit of your vision and dreams. The choices about work and retirement are yours.

2

Consider Flexible Work and Retirement

Whatever the reason people decide to stay in a job, it is time to change the way we think about retirement. A one-size-fits-all approach will no longer match the very different plans that seniors and baby boomers have for their later years.

—Herb Kohl, Senator from Wisconsin

Myth: Retirement Is a Cliff We Must Jump Off at a Certain Age

Once upon a time, workers left their employers at a fixed age, usually 65, and turned to a life of leisure. Workers who were eager to stop working left at age 62, or as early as 55, if benefit plans made it possible for them to retire early. In recent decades, the average retirement age has been about 62. Few employees have stayed past age 65.

But times have changed. When you turn 55, 60, or 65, most likely you will not need to feel pressured to leave work. You may want to keep on working to earn income, build up your assets, and enjoy your life pursuits. Your options include

- **Continued employment**—There can be no mandatory retirement age in America (with only a few exceptions, such as airline pilots).
- **A change of job or role**—You can pursue a different type of work in your company or another company.

- **Phased retirement**—You can work with reduced hours in the same or a different company.

- **Flexible work arrangements**—You can choose your preferred workplace and work schedule arrangements.

- **Independent work**—You can go out on your own and generate your own work and income, as an entrepreneur, a contractor with companies, or a part-time employee at one or more companies.

As a "free agent," you have the freedom of choice. You have the option to retire from your company and find a new job elsewhere. You can choose and prepare for a different "encore" career, perhaps in a different field. You can work for charities or nonprofit organizations (as a volunteer or for pay). You can try your hand at total retirement and later change your mind.

To make informed decisions, you need to understand these alternative courses of action and their implications. Think of them not only as opportunities, but also as alternatives with consequences, both positive and negative. As you likely experienced throughout your career, your decisions sometimes opened up doors and closed others. As you grow older, you want to be careful in making difficult and important choices. However, you have the benefit of your life-long experience and insight in your decision-making.

This is not to say you must choose only among work alternatives. You may opt to retire completely, withdrawing from the workforce. You may find retirement to be a positive experience—a time to leave the demands and stresses of a working career and pursue other interests and activities. Improve your golf game. Manage your investment portfolio. Maybe develop real estate. Oops—that's starting to sound like work! You'll need to determine the right blend of work and retirement as you progress through the "third stage" of your life. The reality is that you'll likely have at least two decades for retirement and work activities—ample time to experiment, change your mind, and make different choices.

This chapter considers alternatives of continuing work rather than abruptly retiring. The following sections describe a variety of arrangements for work, leisure, and retirement that may be available to you.

Is Retirement Attractive to You?

Your parents and many older members of the baby boomer generation did not consider retirement to be a choice. Ceasing to work at a certain age was considered inevitable and encouraged by employers in order to make way for younger talent. Viewing retirement as an age-based milestone contributed to the idea of a "retirement cliff." The concept was created as part of the design of retirement benefit programs during the twentieth century. The term suggests that individuals lose status as they approach the edge of the cliff and then fall into new lifestyles for which they may be neither desirous nor well prepared. In fact, retirement can leave many older workers frustrated, angry, and, in some instances, poorer. Without the support of generous pensions and health benefits, retirement can look less like "golden years" than a "scrap heap of life."

Over the course of history, workers (many of whom were farmers) typically continued to work as long as they were physically able. They continued working because they had no assurance of sufficient assets or income to sustain them without work. To withdraw from work and shift to leisure was a luxury few could afford. Thus, over time, retirement has become a well-established social marker, signaling an expected shift into a new, late phase in life. Since the 1950s, many Americans have looked forward to retirement and planned for it. Retirement income and health care benefits provided by employers have been very powerful and positive incentives to leave work. The attractions of retirement have been promoted heavily by businesses focused on a particular niche of retirement-related needs (retirement communities and housing, insurance, financial services, travel and leisure, health care, and so on).

Yet surveys show that about 75% of boomers age 50–60 say they intend to work; only about 25% say they will retire and live on their benefits and savings. This is a significant change from past patterns: Persons 60–70 have typically retired (70%) and only about 35% work. Of course, the choice is a personal one. You have the luxury of doing what you conclude is the best course for you in a changing environment and at a time when boomers are challenging and exploding traditional models of aging and retirement.

As an example, at 58, Bob took early retirement from his company in New York. After 25 years, he had had enough, and was reluctant to live through yet another change in management. His house in the suburbs had appreciated greatly in value, and he and his wife decided it was time to make a big change. After a short period of international travel, they sold their home. They bought two condominiums, one on the New England coast and one in Florida. They divide their time between the two and have built friendships, found new activities, and have thoroughly enjoyed being "out of the city." They are in good health and have sufficient assets and retirement income to meet their needs.

Bill, on the other hand, retired early from IBM and joined some friends in a small consulting firm to continue using his expertise in management development and to supplement his retirement income. He also became involved with a local college to help them develop and conduct executive development programs and an executive MBA. He built upon his professional and corporate experience to continue the professional work he enjoys.

Ivana had a unique experience, reminding us that, despite pursuing a dream that didn't pay off, she had no regrets about trying her hand at entrepreneurship. A corporate executive who worked in corporations her entire life, she always regretted not being able to capitalize on her artistic abilities. At age 60, she decided to retire and become a personal shopper for clients seeking the perfect pieces of art for their homes or offices. After a year of running around the country to find just the right works to meet her clients' desires, Ivana was not only tired of the extensive travel but found minimal margin and even less joy in what proved to be a frustrating undertaking. Yet when describing the choice she made, she valued the chance to learn firsthand what it was like to be an entrepreneur. Rather than living her life without ever knowing if she passed up actualizing on her true passion, she returned contently to the corporate world as a part-time consultant knowing that she'd satisfied her desire.

As the preceding examples indicate, retirement decisions often involve risk-taking and experimentation. They can also result in multiple changes, including relocation, new relationships, new priorities, and alternate spending patterns. In considering when or whether to retire, you might consider these factors:

- Will your retirement income/financial resources for retirement be adequate?
- Are your peers and colleagues retiring or are you the only one considering this alternative?
- Are leisure and other activities even more attractive to you than work?
- Is your work physically demanding, stressful, or otherwise unpleasant?
- Do you face issues of poor or declining health?
- Is your spouse or partner interested in retirement and the opportunities it offers?
- Are you experiencing age discrimination, whether overt or subtle, in your workplace?
- Are few opportunities available for you to continue working—whether due to job scarcity, obsolescence or narrowness of your skills, or competition with others for work?
- Are you bored with what you have been doing and ready to explore alternatives?
- Do you have an unrealized dream in mind—something you've always wanted to pursue—and are now ready to explore possibilities?

Many people say yes to these questions. In recent decades, most people have opted to live longer in retirement rather than to extend their working careers. During the 1960s, there was a widespread belief that automation and improved productivity in America would enable older adults to stop working and instead enjoy leisure activities. The young baby boom generation promised to take over the working roles and to drive economic growth and prosperity that would permit a good lifestyle for all. The strong economy made retirement attractive. Retirement communities cropped up in Florida, California, and Arizona. AARP (then called the American Association of Retired Persons) expanded as a voice for the growing retired population and as a provider of services to them. Now those young boomers are facing their own retirement decisions.

Employees covered by a defined benefit pension program and a retirement health care plan are more likely to take retirement than those who are not. Those covered under defined benefit pension plans often have an incentive to leave their employer as soon as they are retirement eligible (for example, age 55) and work elsewhere. They can begin to collect their pension, which often includes an increased supplemental early retirement benefit, while also earning a salary at another employer.

Yet the decision to retire is not always voluntary. Many employers have encouraged older workers to retire as a means of reshaping or downsizing their workforce. A study by MetLife found that among persons age 55–59 who retired, the two most frequently cited reasons were: "offered an early retirement package (36%) and business closed/downsized (17%)." When retirements are "encouraged," individuals are less likely to have thought through their options or made plans for their future. In many cases, these retirees end up returning to the workforce in order to supplement their (inadequate) retirement income.

The trend-setting baby boomer generation is challenging traditional notions of retirement and exploring alternative ways to remain engaged in the world of work. The idea of a "normal" retirement at a certain age will no longer be relevant. More are staying in the workforce than the previous generation. MetLife's research revealed trends toward later retirement, reflecting a wider variety of work and retirement patterns among persons in the age group of older baby boomers.

Asked whether their concept of retirement had changed, 47% of older boomers (55–59) said "yes." As leading-edge boomers make their own career choices and pursue alternate paths, younger boomers will likely follow, significantly changing the landscape of work and retirement.

—MetLife, 2006

Why Continue Working?

Why retire? Why should you step aside for others to take your place? Why should you "drop out"? Given projections that you and your peers can expect to live long into your nineties, how realistic is it for you to think about retirement before age 65 or 70? The most satisfying and productive years of your life may lie ahead. You can take advantage of your accumulated professional talents and career accomplishments, your experience in a variety of organizations and industries, and your motivation to pursue interesting work and to ensure greater financial security.

MetLife's research found the primary reason individuals age 60–65 retired was that they "wanted to try something new and different." New life patterns will allow for the continuous reinvention, ongoing improvement, and choice of work throughout one's life. You may find your desire to "rewire rather than retire" is a primary factor in your decisions. When you have ten or twenty active years ahead, what will you want to do? Answer: something meaningful.

The boomer generation will swell the over-age-60 segment of the population to 70 million over the next 20 years. Today, turning age 55, 60, or 65 has less significance as a turning point for boomers, who are generally in better health, enjoy their work more, and are more eager to keep earning money more than previous generations. Retirement age is no longer meaningful as many boomers reject retirement as an event and instead move in and out of the workforce until they are 70, 75, or older. There will be no retirement age cliff.

Instead of reaching a retirement age that might signal a loss of meaningful roles or human relationships, you may cycle in and out of a career, take breaks in between, and develop new capabilities. You will likely move in and out of periods of work while also devoting time to learning and leisure and personal interests as you choose. The traditional model of life stages—learning in school, then working, then retiring to leisure—is not likely to be relevant for many boomers. You can instead "shuffle" your life stages so that you return to education and develop new talents several times in your life; you may take time for leisure between jobs or periods of intense work. Indeed, many boomers are already working as free agents—providing consulting or services to clients on a project basis, permitting them to work hard, then play hard, and continually reinvent their "personal brand."

Generation X and Y employees are expecting employers to provide more work-life flexibility, including work hours, time away from work, and sabbaticals and leaves. Boomers can benefit from the changes and policies that these younger employees encouraged employers to develop and implement. Women, in particular, have led the way in establishing new expectations for flexibility in work and careers, making it acceptable to take leaves for childbirth, child-rearing, and parental responsibilities, and also by shifting career directions and pursuing non-traditional occupations. Taking time off, reducing work schedules, or stopping out for periods of time is rarely looked on as a "career killer" any more. The federal Family Medical and Leave Act has facilitated breaks in "normal" work and career patterns frequently sought by employees.

Just as you might ask yourself why you would want to retire, also ask yourself why you would want to work. Consider these questions:

- Do you enjoy your work? Would you rather keep working than retire?
- Are there new or different work and career opportunities out there that you feel are attractive and exciting?
- Have you had second thoughts about your career? Was there another path not taken? Would you like to change directions and follow that path?
- Do you expect to be healthy, active, and interested in meaningful work well beyond age 65, or even 70 or 75?
- Will you need to earn further income to maintain the lifestyle that you enjoy?
- Will you need to help meet the needs of your aging parents, your children, or your grandchildren?
- Have you saved a sufficient amount of money or do you have sound investments that will allow you to stop working? Do you know how much you'll need?
- Will you need to keep putting earnings into your savings, in anticipation of retirement? If you have not saved sufficiently over the years, do you want to give a "boost" to your retirement by continuing to work?

A Towers Perrin survey found that more than 78% of employees said they plan to work past retirement age, either to stay involved and active or for financial reasons. Respondents said they do not aspire to retirement as a period of absolute leisure at the end of their careers. Only 22% said they planned to retire as early as possible and would not seek other employment. Of those employees planning to work in their later years, 64% said they expect to work part-time, and most plan to change occupations. These data reveal a decided shift in how people plan to spend the second half of their lives.

Higher workforce participation rates may very well lie ahead as boomers opt to stay working. Among persons 55–64, labor force participation increased between 1994 and 2002. Participation by men rose from 65.5% to 69.2%. If boomers continue to stay at work as they pass the age 60 mark, the trend of increasing workforce participation in the older age groups will continue, particularly among boomer professionals.

However, more employees typically say they will continue to work beyond normal retirement age than actually end up doing so. Today's older workers tend to stop working for pay by the age of 70. As boomers move into these ranks and make their own decisions, it is uncertain whether they will have the zeal for working that they anticipated they would. One of the key factors is what their peers do—you will certainly keep an eye on what your friends and colleagues do.

Most people age 50 and over choose to work instead of retire for several common reasons, along the lines of those discussed previously. Research studies conducted by MetLife and AARP identified the factors individuals considered to be most important. The following are the factors, in order of importance:

1. Need for income to live on
2. Want to stay active, engaged, productive, and useful
3. Want the opportunity for meaningful work
4. Want to maintain lifestyle, and do things that are enjoyable
5. Need to build additional retirement savings
6. Want to enjoy the social interaction with other people
7. Need to retain or acquire health insurance benefits

The factors that drive your own decision will, of course, reflect your personal desires, knowledge of options, and circumstances. It is clear, however, that the forces driving individuals to stay at work are compelling and reflect a combination of economic, social, and personal factors.

Additional studies show that working to an older age has positive physical and psychological effects. Older employees who work in low-stress jobs with the hours they desire experience better health. Studies at Boston College found that, contrary to popular wisdom, even physically demanding jobs may have a positive effect on the physical health of older workers. Staying active is very important. For many persons, work is fundamental to our personal identity and self-worth. On the other hand, studies show that retirement continues to provide freedom to pursue other activities or interests that may have similar positive effects. The conclusion? Stay active, and you'll stay healthy and happy.

> *Anyone I know that is in the workforce over 65 will say that both the challenge and the mental stimulation is a huge part of maintaining their quality of life, both physically as well as mentally, in terms of really having that productive and that great quality of life that they feel like they have.*
> —Blanche Lincoln, U.S. Senator

The following sections discuss some of the possible work options that you can consider if you intend to continue working.

Working Part-Time

What do we know about boomer's intentions to work? Based on the many surveys conducted by various companies and organizations, we can see the trends. Today, part-time work is more common than full-time work after age 60. A MetLife survey of persons currently age 60–70 found that 38% were working. However, only 39% of these individuals were working more than 35 hours per week. This means that only 15% of those working worked more than 35 hours weekly. After age 65, fewer than 20% of people are actively participating in the workforce.

A majority of respondents in a Towers Perrin's survey indicated that they expected to work part-time (64%); only 21% said they expected to work full-time in their current occupation after "normal retirement age," while 65% stated they planned to leave their current occupations and move into work unrelated to their career occupations. Most said a change in occupations would allow them to pursue new interests and opportunities for personal growth.

Similar to other research studies, Merrill Lynch found that the majority of boomers (75%) intend to keep working in retirement. Individuals surveyed expected to retire from their current jobs at the average age of 64 and then launch a new career. Some want to stay in the same type of work, but with more flexible scheduling. Many more indicated they would like to have a different, more personally rewarding job. Nearly half would like to cycle between periods of work and leisure.

Trying Something New

Two in three individuals (65%) of the respondents in Towers Perrin's retirement research said they planned to leave their current occupations before their normal retirement age. Of those employees planning to work in their later years, only 21% said they expect to work full-time in their current occupation after retirement age. Interestingly, they do not intend to stay with their companies to continue doing what they have been doing.

Self-employed persons tend to keep on working without regard to their rising age, like craftsmen and farmers in past centuries. However, a study by RAND for AARP found that nearly two-thirds of older self-employed workers made the transition to self-employment at or before age 50. This means that many individuals found that major career shifts (and risk taking) were achieved early, but also that one-third did so later even though the challenges may have been more difficult. It suggests that many people make such major changes when they experience a midlife crisis and that the changes are more easily made then than in later retirement years.

Jeff Taylor, founder of Eons, a website tailored for boomers, believes that boomers see themselves as graduating from corporate jobs to pursue entrepreneurial or personal goals. Even those who continue to work in regular jobs want to do something that expresses their personality, their interests, and their hidden skills.

Phasing In Retirement

Another emerging trend among individuals is to phase in their retirement—continuing to work either at the same company or another company with reduced work hours prior to retiring altogether. A large proportion of these workers are in white collar, professional, knowledge worker roles. Blended work and retirement—often referred to as hybrid retirement, partial retirement, phased retirement, or gradual retirement—characterize the working retired.

Boomers, in particular, are considering flexible options, often combining work and other activities. They are seeing retirement as a gradual process of withdrawing from the workforce, not a single act of leaving work entirely or as an objective or destination. Boomers who enjoy working or who need the income may work well into their seventies and eighties before fully disengaging from the joys and demands of work.

Retirement is a transition that varies widely for workers who follow different paths on the road to full withdrawal from the workforce. It is not always clear when retirement begins, and so it is difficult to calculate an average retirement age. For many, retirement is not an abrupt shift from work to leisure. Many shift instead to a new employer, a new type of work, and possibly a reduction in work hours.

A phased retirement program encourages older employees nearing retirement to remain contributing members of the labor force beyond the time they otherwise plan to work. Phased retirement programs could attract older workers to remain employed and to boost the economy through longer workforce participation by experienced employees. It also expands options for older workers and allows them to ease into retirement gradually, before completely exiting the workforce. Employers are thereby able to retain hard-to-replace, experienced workers.

A telephone survey of attitudes toward phased retirement by AARP found that only 19% of respondents had even heard of the term "phased retirement." Of these, nearly 38% said they would be participating in such a program. However, once it was explained to them, of respondents who expressed interest in phased retirement, 78% expected that the availability of such a plan would encourage them to work past their expected retirement age. Forty-six percent of interested workers said they would like to begin phased retirement between ages 60 and 64; 53% said they would like to work 12 fewer hours on average, if offered phase retirement.

A study by Watson Wyatt included telephone interviews about phased retirement with 1,000 individuals ages 50–70 and was supplemented by focus groups. Most surveyed hoped to work part-time (63%), work in a different career area/field (63%), or work more flexible hours (48%). The survey found that the greatest interest in flexible arrangements was among individuals before the current average retirement age of 62 ; 59% of the respondents ages 50–59 were interested in phased retirement.

To facilitate phased retirement, changes in compensation and retirement benefits rules are needed. In 2005, the IRS proposed to permit a portion of an employee's accrued pension benefit to be paid upon phased retirement. The amount paid would not exceed the proportionate reduction in hours worked (at least 20%). Other changes in the IRS requirements would also ease phased retirement. These include the following:

- Simplified requirements for maintaining detailed work records and adjustment of benefits
- A phased retirement option as early as age 55 (when early retirement benefits usually kick in)
- The use of lump sums as phased retirement benefits or payment of phased retirement benefits as in-service distributions
- Temporary additional benefits
- Separation payments to avoid early distribution taxes

You could also consider bridge employment. That is, find a bridge job that allows you to transition less suddenly into an unstructured environment and to fill the gap between a long-term career and full-time retirement. Rather than abruptly leaving your company, you may continue to work in some form for a longer period of time *after* retirement. Bridge employees find such arrangements valuable as they provide continuity and minimize the isolation that often accompanies retirement. Some individuals have opportunities to mentor their successors. Research suggests that bridge employment helps those who may not be psychologically ready to retire by adopting a phased-in approach to retirement. Bridge worker studies in organizations that offer this option revealed that employees valued having continued activity, a daily structure, and less stress. Workers also reported increased self-worth and satisfaction as a result of their providing guidance to the next generation.

As an example, Harold spent nearly 30 years in a human resources career at his company. He eagerly (or at least willingly) moved from one functional area to another, and held generalist positions as an HR Director. However, after several reorganizations of the human resource function, he opted to move into a different corporate staff group. Although it didn't tap his specialized human resource expertise, it enabled him to stay with the company a few years more, as a transition to retirement. Or perhaps he'll go back into human resources for another tour of duty when it restructures again. They need his expertise.

Another bridge retirement option is to serve as a mentor or guide to new employees who are joining your company. Individuals who are facile at developing others and who possess valuable corporate memory can be invaluable resources. Helping to socialize newcomers to organizational culture, share best practices, orient new employees to organization politics, and help people avoid potential landmines is a way for experienced workers to add value as they prepare to exit the company. Such bridge roles not only benefit the employee, but they also allow for the transfer of organizational knowledge that could otherwise be lost with the abrupt departure of long-term, savvy employees.

Pursuing Flexible Work Arrangements

You can shape a combination of work and leisure that meets your needs while simultaneously performing work that is important and meaningful. Like younger generation X and Y individuals, you can also opt to balance your work and your personal life through flexible, customized arrangements. As you chart your own career path, you will likely find employers to be increasingly supportive—they need to retain or recruit retirement-eligible employees who have special knowledge or skills needed for the business.

Some employers are providing flexible employment arrangements for older workers, including rehiring retirees and offering part-time or seasonal work, reduced work hours, and job sharing. However, in reality, a 2001 study found few such arrangements, and these are ad hoc and cover few employees. Typically, the arrangements are provided to skilled workers with expertise that employers need and that are hard to replace. Employers say they simply have not considered formalizing flexible employment contracts because they have not felt them to be necessary. Other reasons are incompatibility with the organizational culture, employment costs, restrictions on pension distributions, and productivity concerns.

Many people find that a gap exists between the phased working arrangements that they prefer and the roles or opportunities that are available to them. Most would like to stay with their career employer and work fewer hours or work in a more flexible work environment before retiring completely. For each phased retirement option, the availability of programs offered by current employers falls short of what's desired. These preferences, as reflected in the following survey data, frequently impel workers to leave the primary employer and pursue opportunities with other employers, to start their own businesses, or to work independently as contractors.

- Work more flexible hours (48% of employees desire; 34% of companies offer)
- Work fewer hours (63% of employees desire, 49% of companies offer)
- Reduced responsibilities (50% of employees desire, 33% of companies offer)
- Do something completely different (63% of employees desire, 45% of companies offer)

Many employees would like to continue working part-time with their current employers to whom they may be very loyal. However, to make arrangements work financially, many workers needed to unlock some of their retirement benefits. This is problematic under defined benefit plans that require an employee to stop working before receiving benefits.

Proposed changes in IRS regulations could facilitate implementation of phased retirement plans. These regulations would allow defined benefit pensions to pay partial retirement benefits prior to retirement to eligible employees who reduce the number of hours they work on the job by at least 20%. If adopted, the regulations would be an important step toward allowing one type of phased retirement—a reduction of work and partial pension payments—while protecting future retirement income security and the integrity of the pension system.

If employers want to retain their older, more experienced workers, they will need to offer more flexible work arrangement alternatives. If the impediments continue, boomers may pursue informal working arrangements, or simply take retirement and then move over to other employers for work, or work independently as entrepreneurs or freelance, contract talent.

What's a Boomer to Do?

As you progress through your fifties and sixties, you have the discretion to make choices about when to retire, whether to continue working, and under what arrangements. Such choices are difficult, requiring evaluation of alternative options, realistic assessment of your personal capabilities and resources, and clarification of your needs, goals, and aspirations. You may choose to retire or continue to work, or find a blend of the two. You may balance your personal risk with security. You may choose to sustain your career direction and your strengths or you may strike out in a new direction and reinvent yourself.

Retirement need not be a cliff. Through careful planning and action, you may make choices that provide security, challenge, meaning, and satisfaction that will make your life fulfilling. Are you comfortable evaluating your work and retirement options? Do you have the information you need? What factors are within your control (for example, free agent)? What factors are outside of your control (for example, organizational retirement policies)? The choices you consider will most likely be based on your answers to the following questions.

When Will You Retire?

Will you retire early, at normal retirement date, or defer retirement? You may opt to follow the lead of others and retire when they do. In some cases, opportunities shape decisions, as when Ford Motor offered a special incentive for early retirement to all of its employees, and half accepted the package! As discussed in this chapter, the decision to retire is influenced by your health, your financial situation, whether you are enjoying your work and see it as meaningful, and whether you have friends at work. On the other side, your timing will be influenced by your aspirations, your goals, and your needs. Are there things you want to do? Are you ready for a change? Are you eager to enjoy retirement? How accepting is your spouse or partner of your retirement timeline? Of course, choosing to retire from an employer may simply mean you are now receiving retirement benefits— and not that you are going to stop working entirely and turn to a life of leisure. Many boomers will continue to elect retirement and adopt a different lifestyle.

Will You Make a Change in the Way You Work?

You may consider shifting to part-time work, a flexible work schedule, working from home, or other phased-retirement arrangement. You may opt to move to a different job or location within your organization, but one related to your experience and skills. You might take a less demanding job, working "back down the ladder." It is becoming more common (and organizationally acceptable) for managers to move to individual contributor roles—which entail less responsibility and stress, but provide satisfaction. Might you be well suited for mid-level roles? Are you willing to make a lateral move or fill an organizational need that may not be as challenging as previous roles in order to remain with your present employer?

Will You Switch to Another Employer?

You may choose to move to another employer—as a way to find more interesting work, more pay, better benefits, new friends and networks, or opportunities to learn and grow. Or you may move in order to move—to a new location, perhaps in anticipation of retirement. You should evaluate the effects of a change on your pension benefits, retirement eligibility, vacation time, and other conditions. Of course, after you have retired from your employer, you are free to work for another company.

Will You Become a Free Agent?

You may choose more independence and flexibility in your work, establishing a transition toward retirement that can include the amount of work you desire. It may be easier to become a free agent. At age 55 or older, you might need up to a year to land a new company job. And then, if past patterns prevail, you may be leaving that job three to five years thereafter. As a consultant or independent contractor, you may work for your previous employer or others. If you feel entrepreneurial, you may opt to build a business, with employees and a profitable business model. Free agents work independently in different kinds of work with different clients—sometimes long-term relationships, and often serial, short-term relationships. AARP reported that 7.4 million Americans are self-employed and half are boomers over age 50. There are risks in being an entrepreneur. If you want to run your own business, some experts advise that you buy an existing, successful business that you can make more successful (has positive cash flow and growth potential), rather than starting a business from scratch (Zissimopoulos and Karoly, 2007).

Will You Transform Your Life?

You may do something radically different. The opportunities are there if you have the will. Some folks climb Mt. McKinley, some go back to college for a new degree, some shift careers, some dedicate themselves to religious or social work. If you have a passion, go for it. Some of these options don't last long. Many persons longed to travel—to hike in Patagonia, to explore Australia, to tour China, to sail around the world on the Queen Mary. After a year or two of travel, they typically revisit their options for work or other activities. Many books are available that can provide guidance on reinventing yourself; they also provide inspirational case stories. It is never too late to do what you really want, although authors suggest that the major changes are best undertaken early (for example, as a response to a mid-life crisis in one's forties).

There are no perfect choices. Your decisions will by necessity be made based on limited knowledge and your sense of what the future holds. Indeed, rather than seeing decisions as forced choices, you may well seek a dynamic balance among a variety of alternatives. Of course, you can change direction frequently, as many boomers have done throughout their careers. Work and retirement are not opposites, but like the Chinese concepts of Yin and Yang, they may be complementary. Aging need not necessarily mean decline and withdrawal; it may also mean growth, exploration, and discovery. The important thing is that you approach your choices with a positive attitude and enthusiasm.

What Is Your Life Timeline?

Draw a line and mark your current age at the left. Assuming you have the possibility of living to 100, how do you envision your future life phases? Given your health and your family genes, do you expect to be healthy and active until you are 80 or 85 (mark your expected age on the line)? Many boomers do. Next, mark when you expect to stop working and earning income, whether it's age 65, 70, or 75. Guess what's left: ten or fifteen bonus years for an active "retirement." You don't have to plan your whole life right now; however, you should look ahead in one-year, five-year, and ten-year increments—laying out blocks of time within which to identify what you hope to be doing. For example, if you are considering starting a business, remember that it can take five to ten years to get established and be profitable. Also, you'll need to consider your financial plan, your health, and other factors affecting your life choices, discussed in the chapters that follow.

Live Well and Pay the Bills

When you were young, you wanted to live forever.
Now you're afraid you just might.
—Wachovia Securities advertisement

Myth: Boomers Can Afford to Retire

As a boomer professional, you are likely counting on pension, savings, and health programs from your employer to sustain you in your retirement, whenever that occurs. Combined with your personal savings and social security, you reasonably expect retirement to be an enjoyable and secure phase of your life.

However, boomers often underestimate their financial needs and overestimate their prospective retirement resources. Research and experience suggest that you need to take a fresh look at your financial situation and plans so that you can live well and pay the bills for decades in your future.

This chapter provides information that will help you think about your retirement income requirements, your prospective retirement income and assets, and gaps that you may need to bridge either through working, saving and investing more, or by adjusting your spending. Viewpoints typically expressed by boomer professionals highlight several sections, followed by factual information that will prompt your thinking about choices you need to make. This information may be astonishing news for you. Or you may have heard of these trends but did not fully consider their implications for your personal financial planning.

Determining Your Living Expenses

"I am targeting income of 80% of my pre-retirement income to support my needs once I retire." Actually, you may find that your boomer lifestyle will require more disposable income than less. If retirement is your chance to enjoy the good life, you should target higher income.

Your first question should be, "How much income do I need to live well for the rest of my life?" The answer depends on your specific needs and the standard of living you seek to maintain. When you retire, your lifestyle and associated spending patterns may change. To answer the question, you could start from scratch and project what you anticipate your living expenses will be when you retire. Will you be living in the same city or same house? Look at what you are spending today and project to the future what you expect you will spend in retirement. Typical spending categories are the following:

- Health care insurance and out-of pocket medical and health care expenses
- Housing (rent or mortgage, taxes, maintenance, insurance, and so on)
- Food
- Personal care
- Transportation (car payments, insurance, maintenance, other transportation)
- Care of family members (elderly parents, children, and so on)
- Travel
- Entertainment and hobbies
- Charitable gifts
- Fee and tuition for education and lifelong learning
- Other expenses and miscellaneous contingencies

These categories are listed approximately in order of importance—or degree to which they are basic, fixed expenses versus variable, discretionary expenses. These estimates can give you the starting point in creating a budget to guide your spending when you retire, and will give you a reference point in evaluating the adequacy of your retirement income and assets. Health care is important in boomers' minds because of the rising costs and the potential need for health care or long-term care.

You may think that your life will be simpler and less costly after retirement or if you work less. Certain living expenses may be lower or eliminated, such as commuting, business clothing, non-reimbursed travel and entertainment expenses, income taxes, life insurance premiums, and savings. Boomers' parents tended to reduce their costs of living upon retirement. They kept the same car, television, hi-fi, and other things they had for 20 or more years. Most expected to cut back on vacations, travel, and major purchases. Consequently, the conventional wisdom they conveyed is that you should plan on retirement spending to be equivalent to 70% to 80% of your pre-retirement levels.

Lifestyle Spending

You may not want to change your consumer habits when you retire. Boomers, especially professionals, have demonstrated a tendency to spend freely and enjoy the good life they have been accustomed to. Many feel that this is their time to "let loose" and enjoy life more because they cannot anticipate how long they will live. Rather than thinking about leaving money for children or charities that they supported in the past, many are prepared to focus on themselves. Boomers are a consumer generation like none before it. Also, you may be active, with high living expenses well into your seventies, far longer than your parents imagined.

It is reasonable to expect that you will spend *more*, rather than less in retirement. Early in your retirement, you may satisfy pent-up desires for traveling, remodeling, relocating, buying a boat, or other activities that involve new expenses. And even small but frequent spending habits are significant. Remember the "latte" factor: If you buy a Starbuck's latte every day, over the years it adds up to thousands of dollars!

Given what we're learning from boomers who have already retired, a target of 100 to 125% of your income may be a more realistic goal for your retirement, particularly in your early retirement years. As you grow weary of discretionary or costly leisurely activities and choose to "settle down" into a quieter retirement routine, your expenses may decline. But this may not happen until you are age 75 or later.

> *My suggestion is to assume that you'll need a 100% replacement rate. If you end up having more than you actually need, you'll be in better shape.*
>
> —Olivia Mitchell, Professor and Director, Pension Research Council, Wharton School, University of Pennsylvania

Are you willing to change your lifestyle and future plans in order to reduce costs? Are you ready to downsize? Your financial planning needs to be based on your lifestyle and needs. If you know where you will be living in retirement and have a plan for what you will be doing, you can adjust your plans for annual spending. Focus first on what is important to you and what your expenses will be. Then you can adjust your plans to match the income you have available.

Joanne, for example, realized that a large portion of what she was spending was related to keeping up with what her friends were doing. In addition, she entertained work colleagues at her home and often treated her employees to meals in appreciation for their efforts. She realized that such discretionary spending, when totaled, represented a significant amount of money which she could not afford to lay out once retired. Although she remains in touch with former colleagues and coworkers, she now hosts potlucks instead of footing the bill herself. In addition, she no longer has to keep up with the Joneses because they also retired and discovered that they also have less ability to spend at will.

You may face a complicating factor that is becoming very common for boomers: the three-generation "sandwich." Frank is supporting a 90-year-old mother still living in her own home, while also caring for a son in high school and two daughters in college. "How am I supposed to be putting money away, when we're doing all this? For many boomers, the sandwich drains resources at just the time that retirement assets should be accumulating most rapidly—in the years during which earnings usually peak. Today, nearly 50% of people in their sixties have at least one parent who is still alive, versus 7% or fewer a century ago. The cost of residing in a senior living facility ranges from $5,000 to $10,000 per month. It is far less costly to support seniors living in their home. Also many elder services are now available in communities to enable, indeed encourage, seniors to remain in their homes as long as possible.

Additionally, nearly half of all families today have a child older than age 18 living at home at one time or another. For some boomers this is attractive, keeping the family close and involved. Others consider this to be a good reason to downsize and move to a condominium. There are clearly advantages and disadvantages for parents, just as there are for the adult children.

Health Care

"Until we get national health care reform, it looks like we'll have to pay more and more on our own." Health care will be a significant factor for many boomers. Costs have risen significantly and continue to rise.

While many boomers may be covered by company-paid health care benefits after they leave employment, this benefit may not continue. An AARP study showed that 40% of large employers provided retiree health benefits in 1993; however, by 2001 this had fallen to 23%. Further, boomers who shift to part-time or contract work often find themselves without employer plans and are on their own.

Many people are concerned about paying for medical care and outliving their savings/retirement funds. Watson Wyatt projected that future retirees will shoulder substantially more, if not all, of the costs of their health care in retirement. The firm estimates that the level of employer financial support will drop to less than 10% of total retiree medical expense by the year 2031. Instead, companies are working to focus retiree coverage on Medicare programs.

Medicare is becoming the primary health care insurance plan for most boomers. Compared to privately subscribed insurance, it is cost effective because it is subsidized by the government. Yet premiums for Medicare, supplemental insurance coverage, and Part D drug program coverage are all rising and are projected to continue to rise. Further, the Part D drug program has a big "doughnut hole" coverage gap, in which individuals must pay 100% of their drug costs until they meet a preset limit. This adds to personal costs, especially if the gap is hit every year.

Fidelity Investments has predicted that a 65-year old husband and wife would need $200,000 in savings or retirement income to cover medical costs in retirement, assuming they live to age 82 and 85, respectively. This includes premiums for Medicare's doctor and drug coverage (Parts B and D), co-payments, deductibles, other expenses not covered, and out-of pocket drug costs. The estimate does not include long-term care, over-the-counter medicine, or most dental work.

To ease the burden of increased costs on employees and help them prepare for retirement, many companies and insurers have instituted health savings accounts (HSAs) for employees. These health plans combine a low-cost, high-deductible insurance policy with a tax-free savings account.

Long-Term Care

"I am not sure I really need long-term care insurance. I get conflicting messages." Given increased longevity, some boomers are considering whether they should purchase long-term care insurance.

While only about 4% of people age 65 and older are in long-term care facilities, statistics suggest that 25% to 50% of elderly people will need some form of long-term care. Because Medicare does not cover such care, many boomers ask whether they will have the money to pay for health care when they can no longer live independently. Although this is a long-term worry, some purchase long-term care insurance policies that cover home care, assisted living, or nursing-home care. Those who are covered today draw on their policies for about four years, on average.

Until recently, long-term care policies were expensive and complicated and left the insured exposed to big costs (payments per day were far less than actual nursing home costs). Today, costs of long-term care range from $50,000 a year for home care to $75,000 or more for care in facilities. Insurers now offer simplified policies that include inflation protection, guarantees against premium increases, and easier application processes. An annual insurance premium of $3,000 or more may be a prudent investment for many individuals who want to avoid a risk of high long-term care expenses for themselves or for aging parents. On the other hand, younger persons may be reluctant to make payments for years with uncertainty as to the realized value or payoff; the money might better be invested over the years. If a person signs up when he is age 55 older, the policies are more costly and applicants may not qualify due to health conditions. A detailed guide for buyers of long-term care insurance is available from the National Association of Insurance Commissioners (NAIC, 2003). You may also visit the website of the Family Caregiver Alliance in San Francisco for information (www.caregiver.org).

Policies are best suited for people with net assets in the range of $500,000 and $2 million who may want to protect assets for their children. If you have sufficient retirement assets ($2 million or more), you might be better off self-insuring for your long-term care by paying costs out of your retirement assets.

If you are worried that you might outlive your assets, you might consider a new alternative: longevity insurance. Essentially a deferred annuity, a lump sum payment of $50,000 at age 55 may yield income of $44,000 a year starting at age 85, should you live so long.

Determining Income Sources

The longer you continue working and postpone retirement, the better off you will be financially. Working an additional five or ten years makes a significant difference in the level of accumulated assets. It means you are contributing to savings, letting your invested savings grow, and most importantly, you are not drawing them down. In many cases, your social security and pension benefits will be greater if you defer receiving them. If it is clear that you do not have sufficient retirement income or assets, you will be pressed to continue working. Even if you feel that you have ample assets, retirement will likely be more attractive when it is blended with working, earning, traveling, and new pursuits.

Mary has worked at her company for 22 years, and considers it a "second home" with friends and interesting challenges. At age 58, she is in "no rush to retire." At 60, she has the option to retire with a pension, but she plans to wait until she is at least 65, because the pension will be larger, she'll have more cash in her 401(k), and simply "it's a great place to be."

Chuck, on the other hand, has been an independent consultant for twelve years, since leaving IBM when it closed his business division. Although traveling is getting difficult to tolerate, the clients and projects are gratifying. The income goes up and down, but the variable work means he has time for him and his wife to spend with their children and grandchildren. "I don't see myself taking down my shingle. I'll keep on consulting as long as the phone rings. Every buck I earn is a buck I don't have to take out of my savings."

In addition to earnings, you may rely on three traditional sources of retirement income: social security, pension, and personal savings (including direct savings and IRA/401(k) plans). Boomers indicate that they will rely more on social security benefits and traditional pensions than do younger, next-generation workers. Younger workers are less likely to count on pensions and are turning to personal investments in stocks, bonds, and mutual funds, including those in their company-sponsored retirement savings plans. Many employer pension programs are being eliminated, frozen, or supplemented by defined contribution retirement plans such as 401(k) accounts. Only half of all workers in America are covered by any type of retirement plan at work. Although many boomers can still expect to receive income from traditional pensions, others are counting on savings plans, but may have not enough assets to ensure sufficient retirement income.

If you are an older boomer, you may be more secure than younger boomers and future generations because you have accumulated substantial pension benefits, have saved and invested during the long period of steady stock market appreciation, and have benefited from the value appreciation of your home and other properties. In contrast, younger boomers face changing circumstances and uncertainty of investment returns.

The following sections detail some possible sources of income for your retirement years.

The early boomers, people who are going to retire in the next five years, they'll be okay. The problem is going to be with the young side of the boomers, people in their early fifties now. They're not going to be okay.

—Alicia Munnell, Director, Boston College

Social Security

"I expect Social Security benefits will pay out for me—I'm not affected by the changes that have been made." Actually, rising eligibility age and the taxing of benefits are greatly reducing take-home income. And long-term, who knows what changes will be adopted?

Social Security is important for today's retirees. However, it will be a less important source of income for each successive generation. Social Security benefits are under pressure, with program changes being made and the future viability of program benefits being debated as a political issue. The benefits from Social Security have been reduced by more restrictive rules. Social Security benefit payments before age 65 (62–65) are offset by earned income. After age 65, the age for full retirement benefits eligibility has been raised from 65 to 67. Up to 85% of benefit payments are now taxable, if the individual has a specified level of other income. Rising Medicare premiums also take a larger bite from Social Security checks.

Pension Benefits

"My company pension will provide me with a solid income to cover my basic needs." Actually, many defined benefit plans are being frozen, discontinued, or amended. They are no longer as secure as they once were. If you're within sight of receiving an assured pension, you are fortunate.

Some boomers, particularly those who spent a long career with a single employer, can expect a guaranteed income based on the years of service and final years' salary. Other boomers will receive pension payments from one or more employers where they worked long enough to become vested. At the same time, many boomers will receive no pension because they did not stay at any employer long enough to earn vested benefits. This lack of accumulated benefits is a great concern to the most mobile of boomer professionals. What is your situation?

Lynn, for example, taught at a state university for ten years after she earned her Ph.D. Then she worked on large government-funded projects, moved on to several large companies to head up training and development, and finally returned to another university. Her only earned pension benefits were from her university service early in her career. The bulk of her retirement assets is accumulated personal savings and 401(k) savings from subsequent employers. For this very reason, employees who change jobs frequently prefer a plan such as the 401(k) in which balances are portable.

> *Pensions will continue to be important for employees fortunate to participate in them. Despite news of pension terminations, financial problems, and other problems, boomers are "ahead of the curve" and can likely rely on these benefits.*
> —Bill Novelli, Chairman of AARP, 2006, p. 27.

Savings and 401(k) Programs

"I have always put some of my salary into a 401(k) program." Actually, you will have substantial retirement assets only if you have contributed for a long time and maximized your employer's matching contributions. Experts advise that you put away 15–18% of your income into savings during your whole career—advice rarely taken. However, it is never too late to save. Working and saving for a few more years can significantly boost your retirement assets.

A Merrill Lynch retirement survey found persons who are saving say they are putting away an average of only 12% of their income. Overall, Americans have a net negative rate of savings, after considering accumulating credit card debt, mortgages, and household spending in excess of current income. However, this fails to take into consideration the appreciation in their homes and investments.

Employers are shifting away from pensions toward defined-contribution plans such as 401(k)s, which provide savings incentives and tax advantages but are controlled by the employees. Employees find account-based programs attractive because they are easy to understand and allow them to watch their retirement dollars grow over time. Actually, many contemporary American and foreign companies have grown without pension plans, including Dell, Starbucks, and Home Depot. Employees have grown used to the idea of putting some of their earnings away, usually matched by an employer contribution.

401(k) plans allow employees to put away part of their paycheck tax-free until retirement. They were not intended to provide retirement for all employees, but in just two decades such savings accounts have become widespread and the apparent successor to pensions. Unlike pension payments, your future income from a 401(k) is uncertain. The growth of the fund depends on the investment performance and the mix of investments. Your choices among investment options will affect your account size over the years and the income it will provide to you in retirement. Also, you will need to carefully manage withdrawals from your savings accounts to make the funds last long enough, but with not so much caution that you need to live too frugally or in unnecessary discomfort.

Because participation in a 401(k) plan is voluntary, millions of workers have chosen to put in less than is allowed or nothing at all. This puts their retirement security at risk, especially when there is no pension. Federal legislation in 2006 permitted higher contribution limits, larger "catch-up" contributions by workers age 50 and older, savers' credits for low and middle income households, and use of Roth 401(k)s. Roth plans, created by law in 2001, enable workers to save after-tax dollars and then withdraw those contributions plus their earnings, tax free in retirement.

Younger, next-generation workers who participate fully in a 401(k) or similar plan over many years can build their accounts to provide half or two-thirds of their retirement income by the time they near retirement. If investments perform well, a 401(k) plan may actually accumulate more assets for retirement than a traditional pension might provide. With Social Security and other personal savings, this may add up to a comfortable retirement income. Yet younger boomers are caught in the middle, without many years to accumulate funds, and unable to catch up by contributing more each year. They are often at their peak spending years (because of children, parents, housing, and so on) and so they face a difficult challenge.

For a decent standard of living (not just 80% replacement), workers would have to save, on average, more than 25% of their compensation each and every year, which, of course, is not a feasible situation. And this assumes that Social Security, Medicare, and Medicaid programs continue status quo.

—Jack VanDerhei, Employee Benefit Research Institute (PBS, 2006)

Equity in Your Home

"My biggest retirement investment is in my home. It has increased significantly in value." The reality is that you have to live some place. Many boomers say they want to continue to live in their current home in retirement. If you do this, you will find it difficult to draw retirement assets out of your equity. You can get a second mortgage or a reverse mortgage but these options have high costs and risks.

Overall, your housing costs may be lower if you sell your home and buy something far less costly or rent. This may be a good idea if you have a large home and are ready to downsize. Larger homes require more upkeep. The recent trend towards larger homes is counter to the emerging "aging in place" concept. A lot of people have large homes, but only live in a small part of them. There will likely be a flood of boomers selling their homes in suburbia and buying one-level homes or condominiums in cities or communities that are more senior-friendly. If you choose to sell, be sure you actually free up funds to generate retirement income; many boomers simply buy another property that is just as expensive. Taking on more expenses, higher taxes, or a new mortgage is not the idea; the idea is to downscale.

A majority of boomers indicate they would like to remain in their home as they grow older. You may tap the equity of your home when you are 62 or older through a reverse mortgage. Through a reverse mortgage, you may borrow against the equity in your home, and the loan plus accumulated interest is repaid to the lender when you die or sell your home.

A household could receive about half of the value of its home through a reverse mortgage. In the U.S., a growing number of lenders now offer this product and, as a result, the loans are becoming less complex and the fees less costly. However, be sure to take note of one of the drawbacks to reverse mortgages. There is the high fee a home-owner must pay, as much as 8% of the home value, which goes for government mortgage insurance, points for the lender, and closing costs. And the interest accumulates rapidly. As a result, these are most useful for persons who want to remain in their homes in their old age, after age 80 or 85.

Inheriting Wealth

"I figure my retirement funds will get a boost when my mother passes away." Although an easy way to financial security is through substantial inheritance, you can't count on it. An AARP analysis of actual data through 2004 indicates that the overwhelming majority (80%) of boomers had yet to receive an inheritance. Among boomer families who received an inheritance by 2004, the median value was $64,000 (in 2005 dollars).

Transfers from parents or grandparents can make a big difference in building wealth and influencing your decision to work or retire. Only 14.9% of boomers expected to receive an inheritance in the future, suggesting that inheritance will remain an elusive and likely small contributor to assets for retirement.

Investment Growth

"As I get older, I am shifting into more conservative, lower risk investments." It has been standard advice for persons to lower their investment risk as they grow older. Actually, to build up your desired retirement "nest egg" and to keep up with inflation, you should keep much of your assets in a growth mode. You should talk with a financial advisor to determine your investment mix as you develop a strategy to preserve and grow your assets.

Do you feel you make smart investment decisions? Many employees, responsible for making their own investment choices, have left their money in low-yielding money-market funds, the usual default option in 401(k) plans. Older workers often held too much money in such funds or in their company's own stock. These choices limited the potential growth of funds needed to provide retirement income.

What degree of risk are you willing to take to ensure that your resources are sustained and will continue to grow faster than inflation? You may choose a mix of securities or stock and bond mutual funds that matches your objectives (and willingness to take risk). You may be drawn to life-cycle portfolios or funds. The mix of securities matches the "life cycle" of each investor—changing with different age brackets as investors age. In this way, greater risk (and return) is taken early in one's career (for example, equities and real estate), while less risk (and guaranteed return) is taken near and after retirement (for example, inflation-linked bonds and cash).

It used to be that younger investors were advised to have 80% equities and 20% fixed income securities, while older people were advised to have the reverse. However, this formula is changing, and you may find it necessary to invest more aggressively to achieve higher growth and a larger return to "catch up" in building assets for retirement if your funds are not adequate or if there has been a market downturn that hit the investment portfolio hard. Despite the volatility of the financial markets, investments in equities have generally yielded the best overall, long-term return and growth for individual investors.

Annuities

"I like the idea of a steady, regular income, but I also worry about keeping it up with inflation." If you have a strong need for a secure, predictable flow of income, another option is to put your retirement money into an income annuity. An annuity is a contract, or policy, between you and an insurance company. You pay a lump sum or a series of premiums that the company invests. In return, the company agrees to make regular payments to you over a specific period of years (for example, 25 years) or for the rest of your life, beginning either immediately or at a future date. This investment vehicle is popular because it serves to avoid the uncertainty of the financial markets; however, they are likely not give you as much income and certainly do not grow your assets invested. Some annuities also offer a payment to your beneficiaries if you die before the agreement expires.

Annuities are packaged financial products that inherently are complex and costly; they are profitable for the seller but entail risks for the buyer. If you have an annuity with a fixed term (defined number of years), you may outlive the income stream (joint and survivor options are recommended by many advisors). Inflation may eat up much of the value of a fixed annuity—large monthly payments may not be as attractive as payments that will be adjusted for inflation over time.

Some people opt for variable annuities or equity index annuities that provide returns based on changing values in the stock market but without stock ownership risks. For these annuities, disadvantages may include the variability, the caps on gains that may be realized, sales charges of up to 5%, high ongoing maintenance and administrative fees, and high withdrawal fees. In many cases, they are less tax efficient than regular mutual funds.

Total Retirement Assets

"I feel pretty good. I never dreamed my home and savings would be worth so much. I'm a millionaire!" Actually, the costs of living mean that this is no longer a status of assured wealth and income. Given inflation, a million today is like $500,000 twenty years ago or $100,000 in the 1950s, based on changes in the Consumer Price Index. Today about five million families have $1 million or more in assets, including their home equity and all savings.

If 5% of retirement assets are withdrawn each year in retirement, the resulting annual income is $50,000. For many boomers to sustain their lifestyle, they would need to withdraw more. This most likely means dipping into the capital as they grow older, gambling that they will not outlive their money. And as boomers look forward to living longer active lives, the risk increases.

How much money will you need to provide sufficient retirement income? Financial advisors suggest this logical analysis:

1. Estimate the total annual living costs you anticipate in retirement.

2. Deduct the annual income that you will receive regularly from pensions, Social Security, and annuities to estimate the net additional annual investment income you will need.

3. Multiply the net income requirements by 20. The result is the amount of financial assets required for a secure retirement.

This means that estimated net annual retirement income (income above and beyond Social Security and pension income) of $60,000 would require assets of $1.2 million. A net retirement income of $100,000 would require assets of approximately $2 million. These assets may reside in personal savings, IRAs, 401(k) accounts, and other investments. Assets may also lie in the equity of a home, which could be tapped as income-generating assets by selling the home and renting or buying a less costly home. In many cases, payouts from these sources are taxable, so that needs to be taken into account as well.

Is the multiplier of 20 too high? Some advisors have suggested multipliers of 10 or 12 times expected net income requirements. However, the higher multiplier reflects likely increases in health care expenses, longer life expectancy, and the risks of lower appreciation of assets in the years ahead related to economic uncertainty. You can pick the multiplier you consider reasonable for purposes of looking ahead.

Longevity is the big reason to consider a high multiplier. You must be wary of outlasting your nest egg. If you were to retire at age 65, you might plan your withdrawals based on a 15–20 year retirement period (based on a life expectancy of around 83). However, life expectancy is an average; about half of all boomers your age will live longer than age 83. Your life expectancy also increases as you grow older. Many boomers will live to age 90, 100, or older. Investment advisors are now talking about providing retirement income for 25–30 years. Additional information on estimating your life expectancy is provided in Chapter 4, "Stay Healthy and Active."

Here is an example. George, age 57, is a project manager in a consulting engineering firm. He earns $125,000 and is looking to retire within a few years. He would like about $100,000 income plus his Social Security benefits (whenever he starts receiving them). Because he has changed jobs frequently in his career, he has no vested pension income. At the income replacement rate of 80% and an asset/income multiplier of 12 (the conservative, traditional assumptions), he needs to have a minimum of $960,000 in savings and other assets for a secure retirement. George has about $600,000 in his 401(k) accounts and other investment funds, plus he has a "mostly paid for" home. George has done well professionally and financially. If he works and saves a few more years, he will be in even better shape financially. However, if he uses the income replacement rate of 100% (not even the suggested 125%), and the income multiple of 20 (assuming greater longevity), he needs to have a minimum of $2 million in assets. This is quite a difference and would require George to do some serious rethinking.

Jeff and Mary are typical of many boomer professional households. They have about $500,000 in retirement assets. They are among 14 million households with this amount or more, largely saved from earnings, often from dual incomes. Jeff is a company attorney and Mary teaches grade school. She is a participant in a teacher pension plan; he is vested in a pension, but only has 14 years of credited service. In their mid-fifties, they plan to keep on working and saving for retirement.

Bill and Janet, however, have accumulated less net wealth largely because they had less income from which to draw savings. He is a computer programmer, working as an independent contractor; Janet is a part-time nurse. She did not work for the years they raised their two children, who are now adults. They are among 25 million families with household assets of $100,000 up to $300,000 who will need to plan very carefully. Many boomer professional and technical persons are in this situation—that is, with hardly enough assets for retirement. Compounding the difficulty of saving, some of these families experienced financial losses, chronic illness, or needs for financial support to family members. There always seemed to be expenses that took priority over saving, even in IRAs. Many boomer families have dual incomes, but even together, they worry that they have not set aside enough money for retirement.

There are some families that have ample assets. Jack and Sue Phillips owned a small retail chain that they grew from a single store that Sue's parents owned. Their equity in the business, assets they inherited, and property investments all helped to build assets exceeding $10 million. They are not concerned about assets or retirement income—in fact, their concerns are when to sell the business and retire and what they will do then.

A saying is that, "To be rich is to not have to worry about the costs of everyday living." A survey by Spectrem Group in Chicago asked households that have invested assets (excluding home and possessions) how much it takes to be rich. Only 22% said $1 million is enough money to be rich. Nearly half said $5 million or more. 25% said $25 or more, and 8% said $100 million. In comparison, U.S. Trust, the private banking arm of Bank of America, considers wealthy clients to be those who have $6 million or more in assets or annual income over $325,000. "Ultra-affluent clients" have assets of $20 million or more.

Overall, the top five percent of households in the U.S. have a net worth of $1.4 million or more. The top one percent of households hold one third of all wealth ownership. In some cases, their wealth was acquired through super-high earned incomes (CEOs, investment bankers, venture capitalists, actors, authors, sports figures, and so on). However, their assets were more typically acquired through entrepreneurial business activities, fortuitous investments, or through inheritance.

Forming a Financial Plan

The core message of this book is that you should recognize that your needs may likely exceed your wealth; hence you may need to explore options for continuing some type of paid work, increasing your savings, or changing your expectations for retirement and your future lifestyle.

To do this, you need to assess your needs and assets. If you face a shortfall, you will need to adjust your savings and investing behavior, scale back planned living costs in retirement, defer your retirement and extend your working career, or redefine the concept of retirement to include working. Do you think you can achieve your savings targets during the balance of your career? Are you counting on another housing boom to boost the value of your home? Are you anticipating that inflation will increase your assets despite the fact that your retirement expenses will also increase with inflation?

A Merrill Lynch survey found that 64% of respondents do not have a financial plan identifying the amount of assets needed for retirement and how to build those assets. On the other hand, those with a plan to build assets for retirement also have a plan to convert these assets to a steady stream of income throughout retirement. Respondents who say they have such a plan tended to have larger incomes, higher household assets, and more education.

Retirement financial planning has become important to boomers. The industry of financial advisors, commingled with marketers of retirement income products and services, has grown larger and more sophisticated in recent decades. Financial advisors are eager to provide advice on the best courses of action. Meeting regularly with your advisor, especially when a change occurs in your life that may have financial implications is a good idea.

A survey by U.S. Trust found that the essential attributes clients seek in financial advisors are that they are trustworthy, understand the client's situation, and keep the client informed. The advisors considered to be most trustworthy were CPAs or accounting firms, private banks, and investment management firms compensated by fees, not by commissions. Rated lower were mutual fund companies, insurance companies, and stockbrokers or brokerage firms.

Financial advisors are important because in all likelihood you have not studied investment planning and management in depth. A Certified Financial Planner (CFP) must take a two-to-three year training program and pass a ten-hour exam. Investments and investment strategies are a major focus in their studies and work, but their expertise goes further. They provide a broad-based approach to retirement, education, taxes, insurance, estates, and other life issues. CFPs can help you plan and manage all facets of your financial life. The knowledge requirements to become a CFP are extensive: Visit www.cfp.net for an overview of topics covered in examinations and other certification requirements.

Certified Financial Analysts (CFA) go in-depth into investment research and analysis. Individuals with four years' experience as a financial advisor (usually a CFP) take the training, which takes four years, followed by three six-hour tests. They learn the inner workings and valuation of stocks, bonds, hedge funds, derivatives, and other exotic investments. A CFA can look at financial statements and provide an informed opinion. The CFA course curriculum builds an understanding of what drives valuation, different markets, and investment returns. Individuals who achieve the designation typically manage institutional money and mutual funds or become involved with corporate finance. Many insurance companies and financial institutions offer web-based tools, advice, and general information to attract and serve boomers as customers. Some of the analytic models provided on the Internet or used by financial advisors take into account a number of variables, including prospective investment returns, interest rates, and inflation, as well as the projected draw upon funds for annual living costs.

Many retirement planning books and websites exist that will guide you through a series of worksheets that ask questions about expected expenses and sources of income. Visit almost any bookstore or search at www.amazon.com. Associations such as AARP; financial service firms such as Fidelity Investments or Merrill Lynch; and media websites such as *Smart Money* and *Money* all have sections devoted to retirement financial analysis, which require you to set a target income requirement. You might also visit the popular "motley fool" website at www.fool.com. You can find a variety of web links for resources at www.analyzenow.com.

Relying on web-based tools, any of the many excellent books on retirement and financial planning, and perhaps a financial advisor, you can evaluate your needs and adopt the right plans for living well and paying the bills.

> *When we are still feeling great, while we have our marbles and our health, this is the time to think about how we want the next 30, 35 years to go. We have to get ourselves out of denial and take a look at the fact that nobody is going to get out of here alive.*
>
> —Ciji Ware, *Rightsizing Your Life*

4

Stay Healthy and Active

To me, old age is always fifteen years older than I am.
—Bernard M. Baruch

Myth: Capabilities That Decline with Age Impede Work Performance

There is no health reason why boomer professionals should not be able to continue working through their sixties and seventies. This can be the best period of your life—a time when you have health, wisdom, experience, less stress from career, and fewer family pressures.

It's true that our physical and mental abilities peak in our twenties and diminish thereafter. Everybody knows it. It's irrefutable. But that's only part of the story. You are not going to fade away anytime soon nor are your capacities going to diminish suddenly:

- Changes that accompany aging are very gradual and vary widely among individuals.
- Your performance, creativity, and learning are unlikely to be affected significantly until you are well into your seventies or eighties.

The big problem is that many people believe simply getting older means getting less able. Some think it means that you have to slow down, give up activities you enjoy, and ultimately give up work. You have to "act your age."

Stereotypes about aging are inaccurate and they are unfair. As a boomer, you need not buy into gross generalizations about your fitness or ability to continue working or doing most anything else you enjoy. Boomers, by and large, are healthy and fit. Research studies repeatedly demonstrate that there is a great deal of adaptability and potential for continued growth, even at advanced ages. Yet the myth persists that *capabilities to perform, create, learn, and contribute decline with age.*

There are basic facts about aging that you and other boomers need to understand and accept. If you do, you'll be able to grow older with greater confidence that you're doing just fine.

- Some changes you experience as you grow older are results of biological processes occurring in your body (for example, difficulties seeing and hearing, physical agility, memory, reaction time). These changes don't occur all of a sudden when you hit age 60; they have been developing since you were in your twenties and are only now starting to become apparent to you. For professional, managerial, and technical work activities, such physical changes are not likely to be impediments for you.

- Many of the changes that occur with aging can be delayed or lessened in effect. You can benefit from your own efforts to maintain your health through nutrition, exercise, hygiene, and health care. You can keep your mental and physical agility, fight disease, and sustain your health by maintaining your fitness, managing stress, reducing body fat, and avoiding substance abuse. Your lifestyle and environment play big roles in shaping your future fitness. You can be among the boomers who are most fit and active.

Biologically, the apparent effects of aging are the result of damage to mitochondria, small particles in cells that control your cell reproduction. The damage causes free radical oxidation, cancer, and other "deadly sins." These develop very slowly and vary widely among individuals. Given advances in biotechnology expected in the decades ahead, such damage may be reversed or prevented through biotech interventions in DNA. As explained in a recent book, *End of Aging*, (deGrey and Rae, 2007), the result will be longer life and sustained health. Of course, research takes time and so, as a boomer, you may or may not benefit personally from such breakthroughs.

As we grow older, some physical and mental capacities diminish, while others stabilize or improve. However, there is no universal pattern of aging. Individual circumstances dictate the rate of decline and whether specific capabilities are relevant to staying active. As a result, chronological age itself is not a useful measure of capabilities and should not be a consideration in work or retirement decisions.

Age is an issue of mind over matter. If you don't mind, it doesn't matter.

—Mark Twain

This chapter summarizes the changes in your physical and mental capacities that you may experience as you grow older. The discussion is based on a large and growing body of research and knowledge on the aging process. Armed with this information, you can make intelligent choices to enhance your health and longevity.

Life Expectancy?

Boomers are likely to live longer and healthier than any previous generation. In 1900, only 13% of 65-year-olds were expected to reach 85; today nearly 50% of today's 65-year-old persons can expect to live that long. Statistical forecasts by the National Institute on Aging project that life expectancy in the U.S. will continue to rise, and people in each generation will remain healthy and capable longer in their lives. Many individuals are likely to reach 100 years age. In turn, baby boomers are more likely to be fit and healthy and will extend their active and working years.

Life expectancy tables (technically called actuarial life or period life tables) are updated and published regularly by the Social Security Administration (www.ssa.gov). They are updated based on the rates of deaths in the population in each age group—which are applied as death probabilities. The longer you live, the more likely you will survive to an old age.

Of course, your life expectancy depends on a variety of factors, including your genetics, medical history, health, and lifestyle. Several websites take you through a detailed set of questions and, based on your responses, give you an estimate of your life expectancy. One longevity calculator developed by several Wharton School faculty is available at http://gosset.wharton.upenn.edu/~foster/mortality/. The livingto100.com website provides a life expectancy calculator using the most current and carefully researched medical and scientific data in order to estimate how old you will live to be. It asks 40 quick questions and takes about 10 minutes to complete. It gives you, at no charge, a personalized list of things you can do differently and how many years you will add if you do so. A similar calculator called the Vitality Compass can be found at www.bluezones.com.

Declining Capabilities?

Over time, you will notice that certain physical capabilities diminish with age. Most people experience gradual decline in physical strength, reduced aerobic and cardiac capacities, slower reaction times, and declines in vision and hearing. There is a great individual variation in such effects of aging and they typically occur very gradually. And as you are surely well aware, there are actions you can take to minimize changes and stay fit.

Intelligence, as it involves use of acquired knowledge, tends not to diminish, although intelligence that involves reasoning and higher mental processes declines slightly. Most people find that their capacities for verbal comprehension and memory, spatial orientation, inductive reasoning, and numerical ability do not vary much with aging. Only perceptual speed tends to diminish with age, but this begins at age 25. Changes are subtle. You may perform well, but you may find that it takes you a little longer than in the past.

Research has found little, if any, relationship between such effects of aging and productivity at work. Some studies of manual dexterity and physical work performance conclude that worker productivity begins to decline between the ages of 30 and 40, while AARP research reveals no significant relationships. With jobs becoming increasingly knowledge-based, loss in physical abilities may not be particularly important to performance for many types of work. The following sections detail some physical abilities in which you may experience a change.

Hearing

Hearing acuity diminishes with age, although very gradually. Of course, excessively loud music and noise are known to damage hearing, which more often occurs among youth. However, older persons are frequently perceived to have hearing problems when, in fact, they do not. Hearing has been researched extensively, usually in laboratory settings. In hearing tests, older adults are often cautious in responding to sounds. When encouraged to take a risk and indicate when they think they hear a sound, hearing results are better. There's another explanation as well. In an annual physical examination, a man asked for a hearing examination, saying his wife complained of his poor hearing. His hearing proved fine, and the doctor indicated that wives often make such complaints!

Vision

Changes in vision are an inevitable effect of aging. Losses in vision tend to occur at certain times in life. Diminished capacity to see is often discovered when trying to discern numbers in a phone book or read small print on the computer screen. Boomers can expect to champion demand for large-print phonebooks, large-print product labels, and enhanced lighting in the workplace.

Some people find it harder to see at a distance or difficult to adapt to the demand of doing close-up work at computer screens. Although visual acuity (ability to see small details) and visual accommodation (seeing clearly near and far) lessen by age 75, most vision problems can be corrected by modern surgical techniques or glasses. Also, more illumination is often necessary as the ability to adjust to light and dark decreases. Optometrists, ophthalmologists, and surgeons are usually able to correct such vision problems. Today, vision is rarely an impairment for productive work or other activities. Although other eye-related problems, such as cataracts and macular degeneration, may surface by age 60, many people have healthy eyes throughout their lives.

Aging eyes and ears do not interfere with our capacity to learn.
—Patricia Cross, Harvard professor

Reaction Time

Enormous differences exist among individuals with respect to re-action time. In fact, some older adults respond more rapidly than younger adults, and reaction time among different cohorts can vary significantly. However, laboratory studies, often the environment for most studies of response time, almost universally show that as we age we tend to respond more slowly.

Yet research shows exercise and good health habits affect reaction time and aging. You can compensate for slower response time by re-peated practicing and pacing of tasks. Older persons are often more cautious about errors and more interested in accuracy than speed, and this may slow response time. Actually, for performance, accuracy may often be more important than speed.

Also, very often what appears to be decline in reaction time or other capacities such as memory or vision may simply be a function of measurement problems and test conditions. Much of what we learn about aging has been through controlled experiments to ascertain changes in adults' capabilities and capacities. Experiments generally lack realism; often, conditions under which individuals perform are ar-tificial and do not reflect real-life experiences. Evidence exists that cautiousness increases with age. Some argue this is the result of les-sons learned based on painful experiences, inhibiting imprudent or less thoughtful actions. When asked to "take a chance," individuals will often perform well.

> *The aging brain of a healthy octogenarian can do almost everything a young person's can do; it just takes a little longer and must begin a little earlier. . .however, this did not impede Immanuel Kant from writing his first book on philosophy at 57 or Will Durant from winning the Pulitzer Prize for history at 83.*
> —George Vaillant, 2002

Memory

The most common stereotype of aging is the "senior moment." Memory has been the focus of significant studies comparing young and older adults. Findings reveal that older adults know things but often cannot recall them as efficiently or as quickly as in the past. Although it is a common belief that older adults recall remote and far distant memories more easily than recent memories, this is true across all ages groups—not just among older adults. Although memory and processing time decrease with age, other cognitive functions remain stable or improve and may offset other losses. Training and practice in problem-solving and memory techniques, such as memory aids, mnemonic devices, and checklists, can significantly improve abilities.

Capacity to Learn and Solve Problems

People learn at the same rate and in nearly the same manner regardless of age. Overall, cognitive abilities and intelligence remain relatively stable as you age. Evidence indicates that intelligence declines, stabilizes, and increases over time, but findings vary according to how it is defined and how it is measured. Actually, among subjects up to age 65, the number of years of education bears a stronger relationship to mental abilities than chronological age. Initial intelligence and high levels of education make a significant difference in performance on intelligence tests, suggesting the brighter we are, the brighter we remain.

Your mental capabilities may actually improve over time. A long-term study on aging (the Seattle Longitudinal Study, Schaie, 1983 and 1996) found that in vocabulary, spatial orientation, verbal memory, and inductive reasoning, middle-aged individuals functioned at a higher level than they did at age 25. This increase was particularly noteworthy for women. Only perceptual speed ability, as measured by speeded arithmetical tasks, showed steady age-related decline. Significant reductions in intelligence do not occur in most persons until their eighties or nineties and then not in all abilities and for all individuals. Counter to popular belief, young adulthood is not necessarily the peak of higher-order cognitive functioning.

While researchers dedicate their lives to studying intelligence, there is limited agreement on what it is and how to define and measure it. Originally, measures of intelligence grew out of a desire by educators to measure academic achievement and to predict its outcome. Today multiple theories of intelligence create new research frontiers, each of which speaks to different dimensions and their importance—such as reasoning, creativity, problem-solving, and capacity to learn.

Research has identified two different forms of adult intelligence that provide a useful distinction for boomers:

- **Fluid intelligence**, which is primarily innate and adaptive to different types of problem-solving, such as the ability to perceive complex relations, typically matures by age 16.
- **Crystallized intelligence**, which is the exercise of what was learned in past applications, such as in school subjects, and which appears in tests of vocabulary and numerical ability measurement.

Older adults consistently have higher crystallized intelligence and declines are often not noticeable until one's eighties or nineties. Scientists believe that fluid intelligence can either be restored or strengthened as people age even though it begins to decline earlier.

At 87, U.S. Supreme Court Justice John Paul Stevens is a prime example of someone whose functional age belies his year of birth, and he has not yet hinted at retirement. Frank Lloyd Wright designed the Guggenheim Museum in New York at age 91. These men hardly "acted their age."

Intellectual stimulation and developmental challenges can make a positive contribution to your well-being as you grow older. Your brain is adaptive and flexible—you can continue to improve, maintain, and even optimize your brain development throughout your adult years. Activities that require complex thinking is associated with high levels of intellectual flexibility at older ages. For example, Sudoku puzzles can be good for you. Completing them stimulates the brain and enhances fluid intelligence. The puzzles require ongoing decision-making and adaptive capability in response to changing variables—and create new neural pathways in the brain.

Sometimes it may seem that Gen X or Gen Y individuals are more capable than boomers in certain intellectual tasks. Evidence shows that this is not because boomers' abilities have declined, but rather because next-generation talent actually has higher-order reasoning capabilities. Boomers have every reason to be optimistic about the stability of their intelligence and the ability to perform intellectual work effectively.

> *We know that the brain remains active—our wiring remains flexible—and that it responds positively to challenge, creating new connections that strengthen our capacity to respond to new ideas and generate them. We know that stimulation enhances our health both biologically and emotionally, and that some mental functions actually improve with age and experience.*

—G. D. Cohen, 2000

Dealing with Age Stereotypes and Bias

Much of what people believe about aging does not accurately reflect research findings and experience. Long-standing prejudices and misperceptions of age-related decline reinforce stereotypes that are simply wrong. As a boomer, you are likely to be more intellectually engaged, healthier, and more vigorous than any previous generation and are likely to remain so for many years. You are likely demonstrating greater vitality, pursuing different interests, and living more active lifestyles than your predecessors.

At various times in history, older persons were highly respected, even revered, in their cultures. For example, older persons in early American history were greatly respected (and they largely controlled government, society, and the economy). However, during the twentieth century, there was a shift favoring a youth-oriented culture. This trend was accelerated by the attitudes and activism of the baby boom generation. Today, a strong youth orientation continues in the workplace and the marketplace. However, just as boomers shaped the culture when they were young, they are now challenging the social perceptions of older age.

Ageism—stereotyping and discrimination based on age—fosters a climate that perpetuates negative attitudes. It reinforces the notion that there is timetable of "age-appropriate" events in life—education, family, career, and then retirement. Unwittingly or not, negative attitudes discourage older persons from pursuing their objectives. They often withdraw into the background or retirement, rather than pressing for what they want to do. Although cosmetic treatments can hide wrinkles and gray hair, many people still feel the pressure to conform to the social conventions of age bias.

> *Our unwitting acceptance of negative stereotypes about age and growing older threatens the development of a rich, vital, creatively unfolding identity.*
> —W. A. Sadler, 2000

Boomers will change widespread perceptions of aging as they themselves change the age profile of the population and the workforce. Americans over age 50 are going to play a larger role at work and in other active roles in society. Older people will be more numerous and more visible. Whereas the percentage of the population age 50 and older was 13% in 1900 and 27% in 2000, the share of Americans in this age group will surpass 35% in 2020, even as the overall population continues to grow.

Variety is particularly characteristic of the boomer generation. Attitudes toward health, fitness, and aging vary widely. Differences in gender, race, ethnicity, social class, and political outlook influence how boomers will develop and age. Research studies reveal that the life you lead as a younger person will affect your prospects for older age. Notions of a universal aging experience and discussions of existing trends tend to conceal individual differences that, to a large extent, are a function of demographic characteristics. Certainly it is better to start healthy habits early and sustain them for a lifetime. However, for those of you who have strayed (most people), nature is remarkably forgiving and responsive.

Accentuate Your Strengths

Certain declining capabilities, if relevant, may be offset by other capabilities that improve with age. For example, communication and decision-making skills—which continue to sharpen with age—can more than make up for other declines. Additionally, experience, accumulated knowledge, insight, and patience may enhance your ability to perform effectively. Older adults typically rank high on characteristics important at work, such as dependability, conscientiousness, commitment, and involvement in their jobs.

You should try to align your activities with your interests and capacities. If your knees are a problem, you logically should avoid jogging and tennis. Take up walking or golf. If speed is critical in the work you are doing, look for other work that values accuracy and quality instead.

Studies consistently reveal that older workers have the capacity to continue to perform effectively at work. Conclusions suggest that you should do the following:

- Pursue work that fits your capabilities by building on your strengths and avoiding work affected by your limitations
- Tap your experience and expertise that is relevant to and valued by your employer
- Approach your work with a constructive and positive attitude and remain highly motivated to perform successfully

Find Out Your Functional Age

Most likely the world would be better off if we were to focus on individual capabilities instead of talking about age, universal aging experiences, or broad trends. One way to describe a person's capabilities is to focus on functional age. When people say that 60 is the new 40, or 80 is the new 60, they are alluding to **functional age**. Those persons who can function in the manner expected of a person age 40, displaying the same behavior, capacities, and characteristics, might as well be that age. There are individuals who, at 90, are still running, swimming, working, and otherwise functioning in the manner of much younger persons. Similarly, there are 40-year-olds whose characteristics are associated with older persons.

The www.realage.com website gives you an estimate of your functional age (your RealAge) based on a set of questions similar to those in the life expectancy calculators mentioned earlier. Instead of life expectancy, it gives you your age equivalent to your capabilities. It also gives you a list of factors that make your RealAge younger and a list of factors that make it older. The site also offers a plan and suggested books to help you lower your functional age. RealAge is the publisher of a popular book, *You: Staying Young—The Owner's Manual for Extending Your Warranty* (Roisen and Oz, 2007).

> *How old would you be if you didn't know how old you were?*
> —Satchel Paige

Focusing on functional age rather than chronological age is especially important for a boomer as it can free you to create your own roadmap for the future. People in technical, professional, and managerial roles who take care of themselves and their bodies by maintaining healthy lifestyles and good habits will likely continue to be strong contributors in the workplace for a considerable period of time over their lifespans. The free-agency model, well understood in the world of sports, could well be the new paradigm for boomer-age adults. As a self-directed individual who views your career and life choices as your own (rather than being directed by an employer), you should market yourself and your experience without trepidation.

The bottom line is that you can accommodate to changing capacities just as employers can improve their ability to accommodate your needs. Opportunities and choices exist for you, as well as your employer, to capitalize on the strengths and experience you bring to the workplace, especially given talent gaps that need to be filled by experienced professionals.

> *We need to think differently about aging. People are living about 30 years longer than they used to. That means that society is going to have older people, and we're going to need different priorities and mindsets.*
> —Robert N. Butler, gerontologist

Look Your Best

In American society, older adults are frequently less valued than the young based simply on superficial appearance. Unflattering jokes, often part of everyday conversations, reinforce a young-old dichotomy and marginalize adults who don't correspond to how people are supposed to look and act when doing things normally associated with a younger age. Katherine, blessed with good genes, looks more like 45 than 65. Yet she is quiet about her age. When her colleagues talk about their five-year-olds starting school, she withholds references to her 38-year-old son. She worries that her coworkers may think she doesn't fit the youthful profile of her cutting-edge, high-tech company.

Although of late the "gray market" has spawned a shift in advertising approaches, television ads and marketing campaigns still include young, good-looking models. Less than 2% of prime-time television characters are age 65 or older; middle-aged writers languish on the sidelines as men under 40 get most of Hollywood's writing jobs for television and film. As a consequence, some who fear aging go to extreme lengths to mitigate external telltale signs. In 2004, the U.S. market for anti-aging products and services grew to more than $45.5 billion and will reach nearly $72 billion if it continues to grow at its present annual rate of 9.5%. To improve job prospects, 63% of job applicants surveyed by Harlson and Parker said they would leave dates off their resumes to hide their age, and 18% said they would undergo cosmetic surgery. These examples reinforce the notion that chronological aging is an undesirable progression and creates age anxiety among members of the boomer generation.

Show Boomer Pride

You should speak up and challenge behaviors that are based on aging myths. Don't let others relegate you to roles they consider "age appropriate." Talk with your manager about your interests, abilities, and plans for the future. Show that you are fully engaged and that you intend to stay engaged and active.

Social scientist, Kenneth Gergen, suggests that people shape their environment and not the other way around. While he does not ignore the role of biology on aging, he argues that we can create our own reality. Such a philosophy empowers you to be an active agent—initiating, influencing, organizing, and executing action plans to produce certain results just as your generation has done in the past.

Jim, a manager whose hair turned gray at 28, experienced discrimination at a young age. Finally, at a company "lunch & learn" series, he engaged 30 people in a lively discussion about ageism. He also spoke about his boomer father—CEO of a major market company—who proudly proclaims that each gray hair on his head is a strand of wisdom spawned by life experiences. Jim and his father showed that we have the opportunity to redefine what it means to age. We can turn what some see as downsides to our advantage.

If you join other boomers to defy age stereotypes, attitudes will change. With a belief in personal self-efficacy, combined with personal navigation—the ability to take control of your life journey—boomers can overcome institutional, personal, and social barriers that impede their self-determination and choices.

Far more than is usually assumed, successful aging is in our hands. What we can do for ourselves, however, depends partly on the opportunities and constraints that are presented to us as we age—in short, on the attitudes and expectations of others toward older people, and on policies of the larger society of which we are a part.
—Rowe and Kahn, 1998

Making Healthy Lifestyle Choices

You should consider the factors that affect your health and longevity. A tool to help you make a more detailed personal assessment is available at the www.livingto100.com website. The site provides a series of questions that lead to an estimate of your life expectancy. You can go back and adjust your answers to be more healthful and see what the effect could be.

The evidence is incontrovertible. Exercise, diet, and not smoking extend longevity and sustain health and well being. Not only do informed lifestyle changes enhance stamina, sustain wellness, and fend off disease, but they also help to promote a positive self-image for those who follow healthful regimens. Acceptance of negative stereotypes about aging can threaten your self-concept and diminish your creative identity. Instead of succumbing to prejudices and myths, take charge of your body and habits so that when you look in the mirror, you can be proud of what you see.

Integrating healthy habits into your life requires difficult personal choices. Books, DVDs, and Internet-based materials on nutrition, exercise, and healthy habits are abundantly available. The issue, however, is not an absence of information but rather deciding to pursue a healthy lifestyle. Triumph is no more than "trying" with "oomph" added! Most boomers know of or have tried purported miracle diets, so-called ultimate workout programs, and ten-minute fixes to firm their bodies. Frequent "gym talk" touts what worked for someone else, suggesting perhaps it will work for you. While there are alternative approaches to maintaining good health, research shows that spending just 30 minutes a day exercising, even in ten-minute segments, is good for you. The body burns fat as efficiently when you do low- to moderate-intensity workouts as it does with intense exercise. You simply need to work out longer, and deciding to do so is a choice you can make. An added benefit is that exercise is an excellent way to relieve stress, which often accompanies life transitions.

Studies show that among all the things you can do, three factors stand out: regular physical activity, a strong social support system, and belief in your ability to handle what life has to offer—and they can be initiated or increased, even in later life.

Research shows that a resurgence in productive output often appears later in life. Although not as pronounced as creative peaks that occur in your prime, this refutes the idea of an inevitable downhill slide. It is never too late to make changes that directly enhance your ability to live longer and live well. Studies have shown that

- Five years after people of any age quit smoking, they have nearly the same cardiovascular risk as those who never smoked.

- Older people who start doing aerobic exercise can boost cardiovascular fitness by the same average, 10%–30%, as younger people can.

- People who started muscle-building in their eighties and nineties have doubled or tripled their strength in a matter of months.

Questions and concerns about aging are most relevant when they include practical suggestions for taking care of health and making choices about your retirement. Practitioners, researchers, and scientists, many of whom have spent a lifetime focusing on issues of human development, can recall the days when aging was considered a disability. Today, conversations are about rejuvenation and transformation.

The following sections offer some advice for maintaining your health and physical well-being.

Exercise Regularly

Exercising as little as three hours per week by walking briskly can be key to remaining intellectually sharp. The brain's long, slow decline may not be inevitable. While popular wisdom suggests that **mental gymnastics** (reading, playing a musical instrument, memorizing songs, learning to recognize birds or flowers, playing computer-based brain games) is a way to keep mentally fit, the benefit of challenging the mind in different ways has been difficult to prove. University of Illinois researchers discovered that with exercise older brains can "rev up" and boost neuron production (neurogenesis), leading to improvement in thinking, remembering, and cognitive flexibility (thinking outside the box).

People who exercise had the brain volumes of people three years younger, proving a connection between moving the body and firing up your brain. The implications of this groundbreaking research for boomers are that you can increase the gray and white matter of your brain to make it more plastic and adaptive to change. By simply walking briskly, you can wake up brain cells that have always been there but have become dormant with age. The choice is yours!

Regular exercise, as sanctioned and recommended by your doctor, can prolong physical well being. Aerobic and cardiac exercise can prolong the decline of (and even improve) cognitive capacities. However, sustained wear and tear from running, sports, biking, or other exercise can lead you to orthopedists' offices and operating rooms. Sports injuries are the number-two reason for doctor's visits behind the common cold. Some boomers are turning sports medicine into a fast-growing field! By virtue of its rebellious nature, members of your generational cohort are fighting to stay healthy longer. Sometimes they overdo it. Instead of winding down, many are overzealously gearing up for new lifestyles and new life stages. Pace yourself!

You might also consider Eastern approaches to health and well being, embraced by persons of all ages. Ancient practices of qigong or tai chi have been found to retard or reverse some diseases associated with aging by those who use them. They bring together a regimen of low-stress exercise, mental focus, balancing, and spirituality. They include physical movement, breathing exercises, and meditation. Benefits include lower stress, increased body flexibility, and enhanced psychic health (mind and body).

Watch What You Eat

Beyond doubt, research shows that you can lower your risk for the most serious diseases of our lifetime by following a healthy diet. You can prevent 80% of the cases of heart disease and diabetes and help avert hypertension and even some forms of cancer. In fact, approximately 70% of premature deaths and aging are lifestyle related. Choosing foods that you like, complemented by cutting-edge nutritional advice, also enable you to focus on your own particular health concerns. To what extent will healthy eating habits and sensible food choices be part of your equation for living well and being fit?

In 2002, the U.S. government introduced new dietary recommendations and created a web-based food pyramid that includes exercise and offers 12 different eating plans. Ongoing studies have expanded governmental efforts to incorporate the latest nutritional science, shifting the emphasis to eating good fats, whole grains, and healthy protein sources. You now have at your disposal everything from organic markets and health-food stores to specialty, health-conscious restaurants, making it easy to find healthy alternatives to fast food. It stands to reason that you would not put motor oil and corrosive chemicals into the gas tank of your one-of-a-kind, vintage car. So why would you put harmful ingredients and unhealthy foods into your body?

Avoid Smoking

Being a heavy smoker before age 50 was found to be the most important single predictive factor of healthy physical aging in an extensive research study of adult development conducted at Harvard. Prior to this research, variables such as ancestral longevity, parental characteristics, or stress were presumed to predict healthy aging. Although the rank order varied in importance among study groups, control of weight, exercise, and abuse of cigarettes and alcohol—at least by the time an individual is 50—dramatically predicted healthy aging and whether a person would be enjoying his or her eightieth year.

Research shows that it is almost never too late to begin healthy habits such as smoking cessation, sensible diet, exercise, and the like. Even more important, it is never too late to benefit from those changes.

—Rowe and Kahn, 1998

Prevent Disease

The myth suggests that the older you get, the sicker you get. In reality, the older you get, the healthier you've been. To live to 100, you can't have been sick for long periods of time. To live so long, you avoided or survived serious illnesses or avoided debilitating diseases.

American society is increasingly focused on health and disease prevention. People are empowering themselves and searching the web for information on the latest treatments, tools, and medicines that will enable them to avoid diseases or prevail over them. Drugs are now available to cure degenerative conditions. Nutritional supplements, hormones, and regenerative medicines are on the market that can improve your memory, lower cholesterol, and minimize the pain of arthritis. Books, articles, and self-assessment inventories enable you to be a co-researcher and co-manager of your life in partnership with health care professionals.

Alternative approaches associated with complementary medicine are becoming more integrated into mainstream thinking as seen in the increased usage of massage, acupuncture, and homeopathic treatments.

Embrace New Technology

Many of the declining capacities that adults experience over time can be accommodated by workplace modifications. Research for Microsoft revealed that 57% of working-age computer users in the U.S. between 18 and 64 could benefit from accessible technology because of mild to severe vision, hearing, and cognitive difficulties. Microsoft is but one of many companies developing a wide range of products to help mid- and late-career individuals mitigate the effects of age-related sensory difficulties. In the Adam@home comic strip, Adam humorously illustrates how accessible technology can help individuals retain a competitive edge at work.

> *It will be imperative for businesses to have resources that can help them recruit and retain older works, and individuals will need tools that can help them keep their competitive edge at work despite age-related difficulties and impairments. As the U.S. workforce continues to age, the need for accessible technology as a widespread and mainstream business resource will increase even more.*
>
> —Forrester Research, 2003

Be Future Oriented

In the Harvard studies, future orientation was found to be a prominent personal quality contributing to healthy aging. This is the ability to anticipate, to plan, and to hope. This characteristic speaks directly to boomers who are taking charge of their lives and developing plans that address their personal needs and desires to remain active and engaged whether at work or at play.

Staying active at work has beneficial effects on your physical and psychological well being. This holds true even in jobs that are undesirable and in positions that have excessive demands or otherwise cause dissatisfaction. It is vital to stay active and engaged.

> *We have barely even considered the possibility of aging for new kinds of loving intimacy, purposeful work and activity, learning and knowing, community, and care. To see age as continued human development involves a revolutionary paradigm shift.*
>
> —Betty Friedan, age 76

Maintain Connections

Whether you continue to work or decide to retire, staying connected to others is important to your well being. For boomers who remain in the workforce and who are notorious for "working to live and living to work," balancing work and play is especially important. According to Carl Jung, "In every adult there lurks a child—an eternal child, something that is always becoming, is never completed, and calls for unceasing care, attention, and education." If you create greater work-life balance while still employed by integrating leisure, avocational interests, and relationships, you can minimize feelings of loss or disengagement upon retirement. No doubt, retiring and leaving behind the "old gang" at the office, especially if you don't have hobbies, can be daunting. Therefore, building a post-institutional identity is an especially important consideration.

Having attachments and relationships in your life and maintaining connections with significant others—friends, partners, spouses, and colleagues—is not only life-enhancing but also life-saving. People who are lonely are twice as likely to have ulcers, and unmarried men are two to three times as likely to die of a heart attack as married individuals. This is not to suggest that marriage is the answer but rather that support from, caring by, and intense bonding with others has the potential to hasten recovery and extend life.

Loneliness is hard to quantify; however, individuals who ranked highest on loneliness scales were twice as likely to develop the type of dementia associated with Alzheimer's disease. This underscores how critical it is to feel appreciated by and connected to others. As you consider ways to make connections, cultivate friends, and socialize with others, volunteering can be a meaningful decision. By doing something that is personally satisfying, you can make a worthwhile contribution while also benefiting from interactions with others. Other alternatives for developing relationships may include engaging in communal activities, traveling with others, taking a class, or joining an investment or book club. All present opportunities to make new friends while also satisfying personal interests and goals.

The research also found that cultivating friends and developing a social network, before and after 50, is important for healthy aging. Many individuals leave behind friends and colleagues when they retire or relocate, leaving a void. It is important to form new relationships—and this may require explicit plans for getting to know others and getting involved in groups. Take care not to cut yourself off abruptly from social networks and friends as you make life changes and make a concerted effort to develop new relationships over time. Follow the example of Gen X and Y folks: Don't let distance be a barrier—keep in touch through the Internet and phone calls.

Manage Stress

Boomers talk a lot about stress. Retirement is often considered an escape from the stresses experienced in work organizations, the physical and mental strains of working long hours, traveling, and meeting deadlines. Often it is the unpleasant factors at work and in other environments that are stressors.

It is common to link stress with distress—stress evoked by negative feelings and events. However, not all stress has negative implications. Stress can also be positive. **Eustress**—a positive form of stress—evokes positive emotions and can be pleasant or curative. Controlled stress can give you a competitive edge. For example, athletes and performers often achieve more and perform better when they experience positive stress. Most likely you've experienced eustress when giving a speech or making a presentation. Boomer professionals and managers typically thrive on challenge, achievement, and pursuit of personal satisfaction.

Canadian physician, Hans Selye (1956), defined stress as the body's response to any demand for changes. Left uncontrolled, negative stress can cause disease, illness, and fatigue. Major life events, such as changing jobs or moving, are changes that have the potential to create negative stress. Getting divorced, being fired, experiencing financial hardship or bankruptcy, or suffering a death in the family are common examples of potentially stressful events. When two or more of these occur at the same time, responding and adapting is more difficult for a person. People often get ill when too many stressful events concurrently. The good news for most boomers is that such major stressors, if experienced, are in the past. The factors concerning boomers most are financial condition, lifestyle and work choices, and health concerns.

There are many ways to relieve stress, or at least the symptoms of stress. Many boomers find comfort in the following:

- Jogging and other aerobic exercises
- Meditation, yoga, tai chi, and prayer
- Muscular relaxation exercises, deep breathing, massage therapy, Autogenic training
- Acupuncture, acupressure, biofeedback, visual imagery, self-hypnosis
- Vitamins, aromatherapy, prescription medications

However, prevention of stress is better than symptomatic relief. By living a healthy and active life, as discussed in this chapter, you may avoid the negative stress that is often debilitating. Get plenty of sleep (even naps), find time for music and hobbies, put variety into your work, and spend time with family and friends.

The most common conditions in mid-life are non-fatal. The way we live our lives has the greatest influence on delaying or preventing physiological decline and diseases.
—Merrill and Verbrugge, 1999

Creating a Personal Plan

You can implement a myriad of options to ensure that you will stay healthy and active whether you decide to continue working, retire, or pursue leisure activities. One of the luxuries retirement affords is that you can choose how to spend your time. Now is the perfect moment to develop a personal plan that is right for you—one that includes selecting life-enhancing alternatives for staying healthy and fit.

Consider the following options, each of which can contribute to keeping you sharp and boosting your performance. As you rank order the various choices, be sure that the alternatives you prioritize are realistic changes that you are willing to make.

Exercising: Priority #____

- Choose some type of exercise (brisk walking, dance aerobics, hiking, treadmill, swimming, and so on). Gradually build up to a minimum of 30 minutes per day.
- Join a gym or find an exercise partner in order to sustain your resolve and momentum.

Curbing Stress: Priority #____

- Engage in stress-reducing activities (yoga, medication, relaxation tapes, music, walking).
- Identify stressors and vent your feelings by talking with friends, colleagues, family, or clinicians and professionals.

Eating Right: Priority #____

- Eat fruits, vegetables, fatty fish, and foods known to preserve mental agility, protect blood vessels, and promote nerve cell regeneration.
- Drink plenty of water and moderate alcohol intake.
- Avoid trans fats and saturated fats and get healthy fats from particular fish, nuts, and oils.
- Consult a physician or nutritionist about what's right for you.

Maintaining Connections: Priority # ____

- Engage in activities with other people to develop social networks.
- Identify ways to remain in relationship with others in order to reduce stress and stimulate your brain.
- Reserve time for family and friends.
- Socialize and play golf, ride bikes, or walk with other people.
- Volunteer.
- Join an organization or a club.
- Enroll in a class and pursue lifelong learning opportunities.

Upon establishing and initiating your personal plan, keep a log. Monitor your activity level, eating, and progress. Be accountable to yourself for your choices. As a boomer, you do not have to act or feel old. Remember, it's never too late to start living a healthy lifestyle!

Certainly, there will be many paths to successful aging; and there will never be a right way to grow old; but the goal is straightforward: How can we make the journey?

—George Vaillant, 2002

5

Choose Meaningful Activities

Today more people expect to enjoy their work, to become better as they become older. . . . They want to find the sphere in which they can serve their values by putting to work what they are good at, using their strengths, knowledge, and experience.
—Peter Drucker

Myth: Boomers Continue to Work Primarily for the Money

An AARP study by Kathi Brown found that seven out of ten workers 45 and older plan to work after age 60. Earning income is a major reason cited, but one in three says he or she will work primarily for a sense of purpose and enjoyment. Most say they are looking for greater flexibility and autonomy in their work arrangements.

If you are greatly concerned about having sufficient income now and in the future, working for money is critically important. You may stay on in a job and organization you don't like for longer than you prefer, just to keep the pay and benefits coming. If you face health issues, you may opt to stay with an employer longer than you might like in order to keep the health care benefit coverage, which might be difficult to obtain elsewhere or in retirement. In a real sense, these are choices having to do with money.

However, as a boomer professional, you are likely to be interested in more than just earning an income. You are also more likely than other workers to be in good health, be financially secure, and look forward to activities that are meaningful and important. These may include work, leisure, relationships with family and friends, and giving back to your community.

Brown's study found among workers turning age 60 and earning more than $75,000, 66% indicated a major factor influencing their desire to work was the need for health benefits; 54% indicated that the need for money was a major factor. Beyond these concerns, there were more positive reasons for working. The top responses, listed below, reflect a desire to find meaning in life through their work:

- Stay mentally active: 87%
- Stay physically active: 85%
- Be productive and useful: 77%
- Do something fun: 71%
- Help other people: 59%
- Be around people: 58%
- Learn new things: 50%

As you face choices about options to pursue during the next ten or twenty years, you need to consider what work or other activities are meaningful for you and how you can most effectively find or create them. Ask yourself these questions:

- What factors are motivating you to work? Is it money and benefits? The satisfaction from the work itself? Other factors?

- What interests you? What are your passions? This is the time to give your attention to the causes and interests for which you may have never found time.

- What makes work meaningful or satisfying to you? How can you expand your experiences to enrich your life and the lives of others?

- How much work do you want to take on? Do you want to spend more time visiting with family and friends or traveling?

- Do you want a full-time job, or would you prefer to juggle several different kinds of activities? How important is the flexibility of your work commitments and schedules, permitting you to choose how you spend your time?

Betty Friedan observed, "The important consideration may not be 'is there life after work,' but how might work, freed from the drives for power and success that have dominated men and women through midlife, serve the evolving needs of human life in these new years of age."

In this chapter, you gain information and insights into the meaning of work and how it may fulfill your purposes in life. You consider the primary kinds of meaningful activities and how they relate to your specific interests and objectives as well as your broader values and purpose. It may be that you will choose a mix of meaningful activities—a life portfolio, rather than a single job or path. The chapter discusses why work is likely to be meaningful to you and offers suggestions for you to choose activities that are most meaningful.

Considering Meaningful Activities

I am a very happy man. I love my work. I work for a living. And the longer I live, the more I have to work. The cost of living goes up and I go on and on.
—Peter O'Toole

Not everyone has the options afforded highly regarded actors to practice their art into old age. Nor does everyone want to remain in a single profession or line of work for a lifetime. Under the traditional life-stage career model, a professional career would progress from apprentice to individual contributor, to mentor, and finally, to sponsor. However, many professionals have preferred to remain a contributor; others have opted to switch to a new or related field and start anew.

Under most psychological growth models, we are supposed to resolve conflicts about our personal identity and self worth, our relationships, and our caring for others (including parenting) by the time we are adults. Then we are supposed to be concerned with leaving something of substance for the next generation as a legacy, and ultimately feel the completeness of accepting our life. However, life stages are not so linear. Every time we make a major change in job, relationship (for example, marriage, divorce, dating), location, friends, or lifestyle shifts, questions re-emerge that need attention.

Boomers need to consider the kinds of activities that will best match their needs during their "bonus years" from ages 50–75. Many options exist, the most salient of which are summarized next.

Professional Work

Conditioned by years or decades of goal-driven performance and regular performance measurement and feedback, many boomers remain obsessed with achieving results. What have I accomplished? What are my next objectives? This concentration on achievement is established early in people's working careers and is slow to diminish. For others, it is actually not the outcomes that give greatest satisfaction. It is, rather, the pursuit of goals that matters. It is the progress made and the satisfaction that builds on the journey that is meaningful. Perhaps that is why so many people work so diligently in political campaigns when in fact half or more are unsuccessful in electing their candidates.

What makes work meaningful? Research studies by employers indicate that certain characteristics of work greatly influence employee commitment and engagement. In the following list are the top factors that make an organization a great place to work. Which of these are important to you?

- Exciting, challenging work
- A clear understanding of what is expected
- Opportunity to make a difference
- Opportunity to do what I do best
- Opportunity to work with great people
- A best friend at work
- A manager or someone at work cares about me as a person
- Someone at work who encourages my development
- A sense of control and autonomy over my work

- Opportunity to influence decisions that affect me
- Recognition of my performance in ways that are meaningful
- Clear explanation of thinking behind the firm's strategies
- Compensation reflects the value of my performance
- Flexibility in work hours
- Flexibility to find time for development and training
- Adequate time for personal and family life

Many people enjoy their career and their chosen professional or technical specialization and seek to stay on as long as they can. Others are eager to try something new. As discussed earlier in this book, employers are slowly becoming more flexible, providing part-time roles, consulting contracts, or phased retirement options for boomers. Therefore, the first place to look for meaningful work is in your career employer organization.

However, many boomers find they need to look elsewhere for meaningful work alternatives. For example, Rick left his career engineering job when his employer restructured. After considering alternatives, he became an engineering auditor, working for an independent audit firm and inspecting the quality of engineering projects. This gave him the flexibility of working part-time and traveling, leaving room for his cabinetry hobby.

Pursuits may include starting an entrepreneurial business, whether a bed-and-breakfast, a café, a consulting practice, toy making, or real estate investment and remodeling. Whether you enjoy raising horses, growing grapes for wine, or conducting retreats for women, the goal is to find your passion and undertake something personally meaningful to you. This may involve becoming licensed as a professional in a new field, such as becoming a realtor, a financial advisor, or a management coach. Or it may involve shifting the focus of a profession, such as transitioning from being a dancer or actor to becoming a teacher, coach, and choreographer.

For example, Gordon founded and headed a market research firm. When he sold the firm and retired, despite plenty of time and money, he decided he didn't want to stay at home. For the fun of it, he bought and renovated a second home on a Caribbean resort island.

Realizing the market potential, he decided to buy, fix up, and sell additional homes. The result: a new business, requiring new skills, and offering new challenges.

Work becomes leisure by virtue of involvement.

—Marshall McLuhan

Leisure Activities

Because professional careers demand so much of a person's time, leisure activities are alluring alternatives. But preferences for recreation or leisure are widely variable. For many, their work is so enjoyable, who needs leisure? Yet with stressful, demanding professional careers, it is inevitable that eventually you will aspire to a slower pace and time to relax and do things just for the fun of it.

In their research on work and leisure, Ramey and Francis asked people to rank their enjoyment of various activities. The highest ranked (in descending order) were sex, playing sports, fishing, art and music, bars and lounges, playing with kids, hugs and kisses, sleep, church, attend movies, reading, walking, meals out, and visiting with others. In contrast, the lowest-rated activities were going to a car repair shop, to the doctor, or to the dentist. Laundry, cleaning house, and yard work were rated only slightly more enjoyable. Few, if any, people seem to look forward to these tasks.

Many individuals combine family and recreational activities with paid work. Artists, musicians, writers, and others engaged in creative endeavors make a living doing things that others consider leisure. And there are many simple examples every day, close to home. For example, Marta was the sports mom for four children, going to their soccer and other meets through their school years. Although the kids have grown up and moved on, she plays in an adult soccer league and has a full-time job as the director/coordinator of her community's soccer programs.

A common image of a retiree in America is the ardent golf player. The more you play golf, it is widely assumed, the better you get and the more you enjoy it. Although this may not always be true, golf courses today are encouraging its regular players to play more frequently because fewer young people are taking up the sport. Curiously, however, research shows that anyone can learn the game and, with effort and professional guidance, become proficient. Beginners (at any age) who have never played before can learn the correct fundamentals instead of continually trying to correct bad habits.

Social Interaction

For many individuals, interpersonal relationships at work are vital. Having close friends or colleagues in the workplace helps build a sense of purpose and establish strong organizational ties. Relationships are also vital because they affirm mutual respect and equality. Affirmation from others enhances self-identity and self-worth because others who work with you are aware of your talents and acknowledge your contributions.

When you leave an organization where you worked for a long time, you lose your day-to-day contacts. Sustaining your networks after leaving is usually difficult. Similarly, staying in an organization when many of your friends and peers leave is difficult. Making new friends and establishing new networks take extra time and energy, and may not be something in which you want to invest all over again.

We want to have a community and friends with whom to grow older. This is a primary reason that we tend to settle in a particular location and focus on making friends after having moved around so many times in our careers. It is also a driver for joining clubs, going to community activities, and becoming involved in nonprofit organizations. Even homeowner associations in condominium communities provide a way to meet others and make friends.

After decades of working, commuting, and traveling long hours, many managerial and professional persons are eager to spend more time with family and friends. They feel it is a time to reconnect and to enjoy the company of others. Long-time friendships that you have sustained over the years become more important; you will also think about friends who have drifted away. High school or college reunions remind us of the ties that have been lost over the years, and we often try to get in touch with close friends of long ago. Sometimes these relationships are renewed without missing a beat, it seems. Other times, they seem worlds apart.

As a management consultant, traveling six days a week for years and years, Don missed being part of the day-to-day lives of his children. Taking early retirement, he put family first, and made special efforts to get to all the high school, church, and community events that were so important to the family. It was a relief to get off the road and live a normal life while the family was still together.

Jim was a chemical engineer, but he found joy in his family with five children, and ultimately grandchildren. He always had an interest in the family genealogy and, when he retired, he devoted much of his time digging deeper into genealogy, circulating information among relatives, and generally keeping in touch with close and distant relations. He organized several family reunions, attracting family from across the nation, with tours of local cemeteries and ancestral home sites.

Some people simply want to spent enjoyable time with others—and travel is one sure way to make this possible. Russ and his wife love to travel and are the first to sign up for cruises or travel tours somewhere in the world. Often they lined up their friends, family, and former travel companions to join them, but they also built a social network of regular travelers with whom they plan trips.

Boomers who live alone may have a greater desire for relationships with family and friends. For most boomers, the preferred path is to evolve and grow with a spouse as a life-long companion. The intimacy, trust, and understanding of how we adapt and change are especially important in these close relationships. However, this is not always the pattern for some adults. For example, Claudia and her husband married just three years ago, when she was 57. After two divorces she felt she needed a partner for the next phase of her life. "I believe I needed a different husband for each stage of my life. I feel like there was a reason for each person." One way or another, we hope to find the social relationships we want.

Community or Charitable Activities

Reflecting the social values boomers displayed in their youth, many are now giving priority to nonprofit causes. They want to give back to society. When you reach the age of 50 or 60, you may reflect on your life and consider what has been accomplished and what you want to accomplish in your next phase. This may bring you to pursue activities that round out your career—including giving back to the community.

A survey by MetLife Foundation/Civic Ventures found that boomers age 50–59 are seriously thinking about work that helps others. Fully half say they are interested in taking jobs now or in the future to help improve the quality of life in their communities. Particular interest was expressed for work in the following areas:

- Helping the poor, elderly, and other people in need
- Dealing with health issues, whether in health care or fighting a specific disease
- Teaching or education
- Working in a youth program

Of those who expected to *work* in retirement, more than three-quarters were interested in doing so in ways that helped people in need. They said that they want a job that gives them a sense of purpose and that keeps them involved with other people. While many indicated that they look forward to volunteer work, 52% said that earning additional income is important to them.

Boomer professionals and managers have skills and experience that can add great value. Nonprofits typically are unaccustomed to having high-powered help and are often reluctant to embrace their involvement and consequently hold volunteers at bay. Further, boomer professionals are not merely interested in being extra hands, shelving books, or being docents. They want responsible roles and opportunities to implement changes that will achieve substantive results. Many boomers want a clearly defined role or job to do, similar to what they had in their previous career roles. Further, many are looking for nonprofit jobs that pay a salary, however modest it may be, because they feel that being paid is a demonstration of their value.

The boomers' biggest impact will be on eliminating the term "retirement" and inventing a new stage of life, one with significant community leadership at the core. That would be good for everyone.

—Rosabeth Kanter

Nonprofits need to adapt their approach to include and make effective use of the talents of boomer volunteers. At a point in their lives, many boomer managers and professionals with diverse work experiences and impressive resumes are interested in serving as directors on nonprofit corporation boards. This service carries inherent prestige and taps the highest-level of professional and managerial competencies. Additionally, many nonprofit organizations need to improve their management, marketing, and financial performance. To improve organizational effectiveness, Boards of nonprofits are increasingly selecting former executives from the corporate world to fill CEO roles. Nonprofits realize the need to operate with a business model and to become more proficient with increased income flows, tighter expense management, and strategic planning of programs and services for targeted markets. Nonprofits are increasingly facing competition for resources, and success is increasingly dependent on continued innovation and growth.

Sometimes people make major career shifts into nonprofit roles. Examples include the following:

- Katie left a 30-year career in corporate marketing to switch gears. She founded a company to import handicrafts such as bowls, candlesticks, and baskets from Africa to sell in the U.S. market. Her aim is to support the villagers and also the Gorilla Conservation Program, which share the profits.

- Rob retired as a training manager in his company. He decided to return to elementary school teaching, which he had done briefly when he graduated from college 30 years before, and found very satisfying.

- Vince gave up his consulting practice to become CEO of a nonprofit organization that builds homes in Baja California (Mexico). He had worked as a volunteer and when asked to head the enterprise and apply his business skills, he felt it was an extraordinary opportunity to do something important and meaningful.

Boomers who are engaged in teaching, health care, charity, politics, or religious work often view their purpose as a calling. For them, meaningful work is defined by moral or spiritual purpose. They may have a deep sense of dedication and commitment (blending one's will with a surrender to a higher will), a sense of discipline (devoting time, energy, and resources), and a resulting invigoration that drives extraordinary levels of activity and performance. Taking on such work requires that you truly believe that what you are doing is good and meets a genuine need in the community. Whether the work is enjoyable to you or not, you will find the joy and satisfaction in knowing that you made a difference. It requires giving of yourself; the focus is on the beneficiary, not on you.

A higher calling, or vocation (from the Latin *vocare*, "to call"), may be driven by spirituality—the quest for larger meaning, a greater outcome, and importance. People often do their best work when they forget themselves and are not driven from within, but when they are in the grip of some high ideal. Regardless of any particular religion, many people find it natural to believe in a "guiding hand" and to feel that there is a higher purpose for them to fulfill. This faith is backed up by a steadily deepening experience of the spiritual life. Higher calling aside, you may experience a profound sense of satisfaction in this type of activity, maybe for the first time in your life.

Personal Learning and Growth

Boomers are returning to colleges and universities and engaging in self-directed learning. Education may be necessary for a boomer to shift into a different field of work. For many others, it is not a means to a goal, but an end in itself. They want to learn and grow. Contrary to stereotypes, older persons are often the most avid readers and students, embracing new ideas and staying abreast of current literature, current events, science, and other fields of interest.

Everyone seems to have a story to tell about how they chose what to do when the time came to do something new or different. It seems that every publication on retirement or life planning has personal accounts of such changes that were meaningful. For example, in her book, *Thinking About Tomorrow*, Susan Crandell profiles 40 persons who made major changes in their lives.

Many reflect an unfulfilled aspiration, a passion, or zeal that could be addressed after leaving full-time employment, having children grow up, or simply after self-discovery. For example, Sandy, the flight attendant mentioned earlier in this book, turned to a new career in nursing because of her passion for serving others, and because this would be a secure source of work in her future. It took eight years of part-time study for her to earn her nursing degree while also working for the airline. No matter what happens to Sandy in the workplace or later in life, no one can take her credentials away from her.

Stella visited her mother in a retirement facility faithfully each month. One day, when joining several of the residents for lunch. Stella was startled when one of the women at the table said, "My fingers are arthritic, so I can't write letters to my family. But maybe I could press keys on the computer. I have no idea how to use the crazy machine, but can you help me?" From that point on, Stella returned to the facility every two weeks to help residents learn how to perform basic computer functions so they could compose letters. For Stella, a boomer with limited computer proficiency herself, her contribution not only brought personal meaning to her life and the lives of others, but it also prompted her to take additional courses to enhance her own technology skills.

> *Boomers are rethinking and revitalizing their lives. In the past, retirees may have been looking for a rest. Today's boomer retirees welcome a rest, but then are ready to tackle new challenges. More older Americans are working, volunteering, and going back to school than ever before. Boomers are moving in many different directions. This new activism has confused the very concept of retirement. Are you retired? "Yes and no."*
> —Walt Duka and Trish Nicholson

The Best of All Worlds: A Portfolio Life

You are not required to pick only one type of activity or one reason for doing it. Life is more complex than that. Indeed, many activities offer a wonderful blend of work, leisure, learning, and social relationships. Boomers who have been on a single track for their careers are typically eager to diversify. Those who have always done multiple things or have been serial jobholders are accustomed to performing a variety of roles.

By building a mix of roles and activities, you don't have to rely so much on a single job or occupation to provide satisfaction. Instead of thinking in terms of work and leisure (nonwork), you can do some things to earn money, other things for pleasure, and some for worthy causes. You may have close friends in one role, but not another. The different activities fit together to form a balanced whole that is greater than the parts.

> *What I am trying to do is evolve a lifestyle for myself. I looked into my concerns and activities, and one thing I did was to re-sign my full-time, tenured professorship. I created what I call a "portfolio life," setting aside 100 days a year for making money, 100 days for writing, 50 days for what I consider good works, and 100 days for spending time with my wife.*
> —Charles Handy

Professor Charles Handy felt he needed to make a firm allocation of his time, and specific commitments, in order to be able to say "no" to some opportunities and to nudge himself to create other opportunities. He first coined the "portfolio life" concept in his book, *The Age of Unreason*. He wrote, "Don't just be a systems manager for IBM, be a one-dimensional character, and become a portfolio person now. I am trying to make such a lifestyle respectable for career people. If somebody asks what you do, and you can reply in one sentence, you're a failure. You should need half an hour."

You can find what you want from different pursuits, rather than looking for the complete job that somehow provides everything (but rarely does). In fact, employers are increasingly inclined to provide jobs that are shorter term (a few years, not lifelong) and fewer hours (part-time, flexible). This encourages boomers to build a mix of meaningful activities.

Several authors have since published books expanding on the portfolio idea. In *You Unlimited*, a UK publication, McCrudden and Lyons (2005) expand on Handy's concept of the life portfolio by providing tips and case examples. The authors are executives who left traditional careers and pursued interests in new, multiple areas. Their advice: "Concentrate on what you enjoy most, avoid jobs just because they're available, and make sure the jobs fit with the rest of your life." The easiest path, they advise, is to have one regular income source (often from a former full-time employer) and leverage contacts to develop other activities. This requires skills in networking, marketing your skills, strong confidence, and good organization to juggle multiple initiatives. It also implies that you should never burn bridges because you may well want to leverage former employment relationships at some point in the future.

Among the many relevant books, *Portfolio Life* (Corbett and Higgins, 2007), is a useful resource that describes how to achieve a balanced mix of work, learning, leisure, family time, and giving back to the community. Dave Corbett shares his insights from experience as a coach to executives and professionals who are moving into a new chapter of their lives. Whatever publications or information you explore, it behooves you to understand the array of possibilities for interweaving multiple, meaningful activities.

Choosing Meaningful Activities

Meaningful activities are those in which you use your skills or strengths to do or perform something that fulfills a purpose. They take many forms and need not fit the traditional image of a job. Many individuals, especially professionals, find satisfaction through a variety of roles—multiple jobs, community service roles, personal passions, and the very important family roles. Finding a desired balance and flexibility among competing activities is important to many.

Many boomers fell into a college major, a first job, and then other jobs without ever seriously evaluating how well these choices matched their interests, aspirations, and talents. By age 50 or 55, many may well ask, "Is this all there is?" At a point in your second middle age, you will most likely wonder whether the work you have been doing is what you really wanted to do, and whether there is work ahead that you would like to do in the future. If you want to work in the future, or have to work, you should select the kind of work more carefully to bring your personal identity and work roles into alignment and thereby increase your satisfaction from work in the years or decades ahead.

Making choices in life is not a simple, linear process. Decisions often evolve from recurring periods of self-reflection and exploration in which we test our interests, our skills, and the opportunities available to us. We try different things until we find those we feel best fit our talents and our purpose. This can be particularly difficult for baby boomers who have been on one career track in a large organization. A more proactive planning approach is needed. Making choices is easier for persons who have changed jobs, occupations, and companies frequently—or who have adopted a more entrepreneurial lifestyle.

At its essence, *meaningful work is any activity that supports your purpose*. Whether work is meaningful therefore depends on the purposes you consider relevant and important. Do you have a sense of purpose?

> There is purpose whenever we use our gifts and talents to respond to something we believe in. Purpose is the quality we want to center our work around, the way we orient ourselves toward life and work. It is the way we make sense or meaning out of our lives. The boomer age has been one of inside-out searching that involves.
>
> —Richard Leider

Your sense of purpose and meaningful work depends on where you're coming from and where you are going. The definition needs to be tailored to your own experiences, aspirations, dreams, and simple preferences. You need to have an understanding of your purpose. What do you care about? What excites you? What is your passion, aspiration, mission, or calling? This may never be explicit, but you need to get a sense of what is important to you and why you want to perform some activities and not others. What events and circumstances have influenced you? What have you aspired to? What have you missed out on or regretted?

Whether work is meaningful or purposeful is really a reflection of ourselves—how we see ourselves, and our passions or sources of satisfaction. It is also a reaction to how others see us—what they value and respect in us. For most of us, our work is meaningful only if it is socially acknowledged and reinforced—the recognition of others affirms us.

Psychologist Karl Jung argued that we, as human beings, are seeking authenticity. Each of us is different—with similar ingredients, to be sure—but with different individual behavior patterns and outcomes. Growing up (or growing older) is a process of "individuation"—finding out who you really are.

Many executives and professionals are looking for a new identity. When asked at a cocktail party what they do, retirees often are at a loss. Part of the exploration and transition process is to find a new identity—one that is not based on a career occupation or an employer organization. Ask yourself, "What are the one or two things that I am doing that I want other people to know about?"

Many people die with their music still in them. Why is this so? Too often it is because they are always getting ready to live. Before they know it, time runs out.

—Oliver Wendell Holmes

Sooner or later, you may ask yourself, "What have I accomplished that will last? What can I do for the next generation? What is my legacy?" As we grow older, it is expected that we act on our needs for **generativity**—a contribution to the conditions for the next generation. How can some part of you that is important be made to continue so as to help others build their success?

Typically, people think in terms of leveraging the knowledge and wisdom that we have acquired and used in our careers. Wisdom is knowledge that has been applied and seasoned through experience. This may be a subtle difference, but it greatly influences the interpretation and application of teachable knowledge. You have the opportunity to pass along your knowledge through mentoring, developing and conducting training and education, and role modeling.

The concern about the potential departure of boomers from the work force is largely about losing the specialized knowledge and expertise that keeps our technology, our services, and our organizations functioning. Organizations recognize, but cannot measure, the loss of wisdom as the most experienced professional, technical, and managers leave, and capturing or transferring this wisdom is no simple matter.

Young people know the rules; older people know the exceptions.

—Oliver Wendell Holmes

The choices are yours to make. Be sure to dedicate sufficient time to discovering what is meaningful for you. You may choose to do this alone or with a counselor, friends, family, or even your employer. But you need to be honest with yourself and make the commitments that truly reflect your values, interests, and aspirations.

Victor Frankl, the renowned Austrian psychotherapist, observed that despite all that may happen to a person, the last and most important of human freedoms is to choose one's attitudes in a given situation and to choose one's own way. A person needs the striving and struggling for some worthy goal. "What he needs is not the discharge of tension at any cost, but the call of a potential meaning waiting to be fulfilled by him."

Further, it isn't so much what you expect or want from life, but rather what life expects of us that matters most. Frankl observed, "We needed to stop asking about the meaning of life, and instead to think of ourselves as those who were being questioned by life—daily and hourly. Our answer must consist, not in talk and meditation, but in right action and in right conduct. Life ultimately means taking the responsibility to find the right answer to its problems and to fulfill the tasks which it constantly sets for each individual."

What is the meaning of life? To be happy and useful.
—Dalai Lama

6

Pursue Personal Growth and Learning

Education is a process of living, not a preparation for living.
—John Dewey

Myth: Boomers Have Difficulty Learning and Changing

When retirement was the expected next step in life after age 60, there was little impetus for learning and development, unless it was oriented toward bridge, golf, or other leisure pursuits. Today, boomers face a wide range of work and leisure opportunities extending 20–30 years into their future. To take advantage of these opportunities, boomers must continuously reassess their goals and keep their knowledge and skills current.

Educational resources have been traditionally concentrated on the young in order to prepare them for work and careers. Employers continue to focus training and other development programs to the needs of younger employees and new hires. The popular approach of rating and grouping talent as A, B, or C players has the effect of concentrating learning investments in the few and typically young professionals and managers who have a "bright future with the organization."

Managers today still openly say that older persons are unable to learn or are not interested in learning. They say they are not adaptable or open to change. Boomers over age 50 or 55 are seen as lacking the capacity to develop the capabilities needed for new jobs or different kinds of work. They are seen to be in their final career stage before retirement—characterized by mastery and maintenance, or less kindly, decline and disengagement. Companies are reluctant to invest in training or developmental experiences for boomers because they have fewer years left to work than younger talent. Even in the face of a talent shortage, few employers are actively trying to retain and develop their boomer professionals and managers

It is a myth that adults have difficulty learning as they grow older. Research shows that the capacity to learn, adapt, and grow does not normally diminish. However, how adults learn effectively is somewhat different from how young people learn. Older persons are often more susceptible to distractions (relative to young persons who are often adept at multitasking and studying with music). Although absorption of information and reaction time may be slower for some persons, and memory may gradually diminish, active adults have no less capacity to learn, reason, embrace new ideas, and adapt their behaviors than younger persons.

The maturity of adults enables them to concentrate on the tasks of learning with a sense of seriousness and purpose. Their experience and knowledge gives them a strong basis for interpreting and applying new knowledge. And they are less likely to leave the organization (lower turnover). They are more likely to be learning because they want to, not because they have to.

Learning doesn't stop at age 50 or 60. Professionals engage in personal growth and development activities throughout their lives. Boomers are particularly avid consumers of learning resources because they intend to stay active, engaged, and most likely employed for years after traditional retirement age. They are striving to remain competent, current, and valued.

Anyone who stops learning is old, whether at 20 or 80.
—Henry Ford

This chapter introduces you to alternatives—opportunities that will enable you to continually learn, develop, and change as you move from one life or career stage to another. Learn and grow. This is a time in your life to do things you never found time to do, enjoy, or even consider. As you clarify life choices, we offer information in the following sections about the many choices available to you. Some of the options identified will most likely hold greater interest for you than others; however, consider experimenting, expanding previous boundaries, and creating a development plan for yourself that can be both personally and professionally rewarding or meaningful.

Targeting Your Learning

This section offers some ideas and options for zeroing in on opportunities to further your education or training. As you hone your focus, ask yourself: What do you need to learn to stay at the cutting edge in your field? Do you need to develop new knowledge and skills to advance in your profession or prepare for a new role? Do you want to meet the certification requirements for a different job or career? Or do you simply want to keep abreast of changes that may affect or improve your work? Or are you attracted to learning opportunities by the social interaction it offers, or the enjoyment you get from reading and participating in programs? Is learning a means to an end for you? Or is the experience of learning an end in itself—an activity you simply enjoy?

Professional Development

If you want to do meaningful work, as described in Chapter 5, "Choose Meaningful Activities," you need to continually develop the necessary skills and knowledge. It is a jarring reality for many boomers to realize their professional skills and knowledge are becoming out of date. Technology specialists and engineers know that the pace of change in their fields is rapid; the half-life of knowledge can be only a few years. Physicians also know that they need to keep abreast of new treatment practices and medicines, but the pace of change is more gradual. In both cases, there are older professionals who continue to lead the way and others who fail to keep up. You may expect to be only half as competent to perform the jobs for which you were trained if you do not maintain or regain competence.

Anyone in a professional, technical, or managerial occupation needs to recognize the need to learn and grow in order to stay valuable to an employer or competitive in the labor market. The environment of professional work is one of rapid and uncertain change and more complexity in work. This is accelerated by rapid technology change, but is also driven by global competition, intense industry competition, and the pressures on management for steadily increasing productivity, innovation, and operational excellence.

While younger professionals may be more comfortable and knowledgeable about computer technology, boomers are typically very interested in learning technologies that they can use in their work. They express desire to become more comfortable with new technology applications that can reshape how work is done. They recognize that technology-enabled work processes are vital in jobs today, but also recognize that technology enhances the quality of life outside of work by enabling access to information, networks, and the potential of working at home. A significant example is the willingness of boomer-aged architects who adopt computer-assisted design to replace hand drawings. Another is physicians and other health care professionals who embrace automated patient medical records.

Karl, a management professor for 30 years, was asked to conduct a distance learning course through a teleconferencing network. He prepared new PowerPoint presentations for all the course modules, restructured discussion questions so that they would be suitable in the electronic medium, and adapted his approach so that it fit the medium. While apprehensive at first, he said the new approach was not difficult and that actually it was rather fun. On another occasion, he was asked to conduct a course in Argentina, and had his materials translated into Spanish, while also adapting the course materials to the culture. In these instances, he was learning new skills to adapt to new work opportunities.

Based on a seven-year study by the Center for Creative Leadership, Deal (2007) reported that learning and development are critically important goals for professionals across all generations. The top priorities were the same across generations: leadership, team building, communication, problem-solving, decision-making, and skill-based training specific to one's field. Curiously, for boomers, computer training was in the top of their lists (clearly a realistic need to keep abreast of change), but was not the priority for younger generations (who grew up with changing technology). The study found that boomers were also interested in learning necessary skills through web-based training. This contradicts a commonly held assumption that younger people are the ones who want to learn online.

Life-Long Learning

Boomers pursue learning for many personal reasons. The very experience of learning may be enough of a purpose. Learning is fun. It stretches your mind, which health science indicates keeps your brain active and agile.

Learning-oriented individuals are curious people who enjoy learning for learning's sake. These lovers of learning have interest in a myriad of topics and run the gamut from avid readers to frequent museum goers.

Your aims may shift as your personal and professional needs change. While many believe that they are motivated to learn throughout their lives, reasons for learning actually change over time. As you grow older, your needs and desires to learn and grow shift based on your life course, health, and motivation. A national study by Cross indicated that approximately one out of three adult learners said personal satisfaction was the main reason for learning; another one in three said escape from boredom was an incentive for participation.

A common rationale for pursing personal growth and development is related to your life stage and a desire to learn more about changes and transitions. In later life, adults engage in learning and reflection so as to develop their self-awareness, consider options, and engage in new post-career, post-family pursuits. Life is about change, and life-long learning is all about preparing yourself for changes ahead, understanding your development preferences, and guiding your choices and actions. Many adults experience a series of "mini-cycles." Each brings its own challenges and the opportunity to learn and grow.

Life events that happen to you or others are likely triggers for personal growth and development. Programs and learning opportunities abound that can not only help you navigate role changes more successfully but can also prepare you to manage life transitions more effectively. Life events are "teachable moments" that enable you to learn in order to help you adapt to change and continue your development.

In a classic study, Aslanian and Brickell found that 83% of adult learners could describe some past, present, or future change in their lives as the reason for learning. Of the survey respondents, 85% reported that factors such as job changes, promotion, retirement, and death of a loved one were motivating factors. In large part, participation in higher education is due to life transitions. Eighty-five percent of adults identified career transitions as motivating them to learn from among eight possible life transitions. This is not surprising because boomers' lives are strongly identified with work and careers.

Empty nesters commonly turn to travel, college courses, or new pursuits, all of which entail learning. When their children left home for college, for example, Marilyn took two years of intensive Spanish at a local college, an objective she had long held in the back of her mind. Her husband already had some Spanish fluency, and so there was mutual interest. They wanted to increase their enjoyment of travel in Mexico. In fact, they participated in a special program whereby they lived with a family in Mexico for a month, speaking only in Spanish. They also felt that, living in San Diego with its large Hispanic population, this would be a greatly appreciated capability.

I am learning all the time. The tombstone will be my diploma.
—Eartha Kitt

Social Contribution

As you get older, you may feel that it is important to produce something that will outlive you. This need for generativity is particularly relevant for boomers, a generation that has long had a sense of social purpose and contribution. This legacy could be your work, your children, or a specific contribution to the community or society. Gaining the capacity to produce or generate something that lives on and demonstrates you genuinely care about the welfare of future generations is often what prompts older adults to adopt nurturing behaviors at work and coach others.

In this light, you may want to invest time and energy to help others learn and grow. If you are a parent of teenagers, this is a major role and often a difficult one. You may also be mentoring Gen X and Gen Y individuals in the workplace. Mentoring of younger people, a role widely adopted by boomers, is a prime example of generativity in action. By enabling others to benefit from your insights and experience, you will likely gain personal satisfaction and a sense of accomplishment. Although mentoring is largely an intuitive process, important skills are involved, and mentoring strategies can enhance your mentoring effectiveness.

Boomers' interest in making a contribution is underscored by MetLife Foundation and Civic Ventures studies. The studies found that Americans between 50 and 70 want to benefit their communities. Rather than simply volunteering, boomers want to lead efforts to improve their environment and the world. Education can help boomers be equipped to lead projects and take on work that will have a high social impact. Harvard professor, Rosabeth Kanter, envisions individuals over age 55 returning in large numbers to campuses to earn advanced degrees. She calls this "higher-higher education." Student dissertation projects would have a social impact; examples might include how to, design a foundation; create new social enterprises; take a nonprofit to the next level of effectiveness; or plan to reshape a city by working on health, education, and jobs. The philosophical underpinning for such ventures—social justice and social commitment—may have broad-based appeal to boomers. Is this a priority for your development and learning?

> *Going to a university at 50–60 could be the norm. Someday every major university will have graduate schools designed specifically for accomplished professionals who want to make the transition from their primary income-earning careers to their years of flexible service.*
>
> —Rosabeth Kanter

Transitioning to Retirement

The closer you get to retirement, the more likely it is that you will think about, talk about, and plan for retiring. As indicated in Chapter 2, "Consider Flexible Work and Retirement," retirement need not be akin to jumping off a cliff. On the contrary, preparing for and experimenting with retirement can be part of a phased approach to transitioning from a life revolving around work to withdrawal from work. This often difficult transition requires adapting, learning, and changing.

As you entertain the idea of retiring, it is important to understand the various phases that you may pass through as you transition from worker to retiree. Although the length and nature of phases may differ from individual to individual, having a roadmap to anticipate the potential peaks and valleys you may experience is beneficial. Atchley and other sociologists have described the retirement transition in terms of phases. For example, a **pre-retirement phase** most frequently begins as you near retirement, gather information, and initiate planning for the future. The **honeymoon phase** is often a time of newly discovered freedom, a chance to experiment, and an opportunity to play and luxuriate in your free time. Although the length of this phase is person-specific, some find that the novelty wears off after a period of time. A **disenchantment phase** often follows at which time you may feel aimless or even unhappy; ultimately, individuals move on and integrate new realities to form a satisfactory lifestyle during the **reorientation phase**. At some point, you may want to change directions again. You will likely try new activities and make changes that will establish a satisfactory lifestyle. Often professionals retire thinking that golf and leisure will be sufficient, only to find they are not. "I just don't enjoy playing every day like I thought I would. It's just too much."

One of the most important takeaways from this four-phase typology, as well as results from numerous retiree studies, is that retirement is synonymous with adjustment. It takes time to establish a footing and get used to new and different ways of engaging in the world. The good news is that retirement does not leave individuals feeling useless or dissatisfied with life. In fact, retirement has few effects, the most common of which is reduced income (Gall et al., 1997;

Hansson et al., 1997). Myths that retirees experience a decline in health because they retire, or that their social lives change radically, are not born out in research. Individuals who make the most favorable adjustments are those who retire voluntarily, experience good health, have financial resources, and enjoy strong social supports (Gall et al., 1997; Szinovacz and Ekerdt, 1995; Palmore et al., 1985). Becoming well informed and knowledgeable about lifespan development issues will enable you to pursue endeavors and undertake changes that can contribute to executing successful transitions and sustaining well being.

One of the most important takeaways from the research on retirement is that adjustment takes time and effort. Establishing a footing and getting used to new and different ways of engaging in the world takes time. However, adjustment is just that—a shift in context and roles. The most common challenge in retirement is reduced income. Myths that retirees experience decline in health because they retire, or that social lives change radically, are not born out by research. Individuals who make the most favorable adjustments are those who retire voluntarily, experience good health, have financial resources, and enjoy strong social supports. Becoming well informed and knowledgeable about the normal transitions will enable you to pursue endeavors and undertake changes more successfully and less stressfully. Will reading a book, going to a class, or googling "retirement" be the best way for you to become an informed consumer of information?

Personal growth can occur through fun and play, often seen as luxuries during the course of full-time work. Creative pursuits such as painting, gardening, acting, or writing poetry may bring pleasure to you as well as to observers. For those used to life in the corporate world, competitive activities or building a nonprofit organization may be satisfying.

Harvard research found that creative men and women adapt more successfully than do their less creative colleagues; high creativity in middle age predicted sustained physical vigor. Extensive research on adults in their seventies who were creative in their youth demonstrated a clear relationship between continued creativity and successful aging. These findings suggest that pursuing personal growth, enjoying creative pastimes, engaging in health-promoting activities, and having fun can contribute to maintaining your vitality. Learning, growth, and gusto in later life are highly correlated with psychological health. As you transition from full-time work, you have the capacity to take a fresh look at things. And as you transition from who you were to who you want to be, you also have an opportunity to develop a mix of new activities, part-time work, or phased retirement.

> *Creators in their sixties and even seventies are at least as pro-*
> *ductive as they were in their twenties. . . .An octogenarian can*
> *still hope to make important contributions, albeit at a slower*
> *rate.*

—D. K. Simonton

Learning Options

You have extraordinary opportunities not only to enhance your professional skills, knowledge, and abilities but also to satisfy your personal learning needs and desires. However, you may need to adopt different approaches than you did in the past. You and many boomers like yourself are learning and growing by "learning how to learn" in new and exciting ways. Although you may know what you want to know or learn, the challenge lies in determining when and where to begin!

You can consider a variety of learning opportunities to address your needs and desires. The following are examples of opportunities you may find attractive, want to propose to your employer, or engage in with friends, family, or coworkers. Whatever choices you make, keep the blinders off for a while as you consider ways to learn and grow.

As a student and as an employee, your learning was typically guided for you, tailored to filling skill or knowledge gaps identified by your employer. Now you have the flexibility to address topics and choose learning approaches that you consider relevant for you. You can identify, define, and pursue your own developmental paths.

Self-Directed Learning

Informal, rather than formal learning is widespread. Kim et al. (2004) report that sixty-three percent of adults participate in informal activities such as association meetings and workshops, brown bag "lunch and learn" sessions, reading professional journals, and self-paced courses. The National Center for Educational Statistics (Creighton and Hudson, 2002) found similar results, reporting that 63 percent of adults participate in informal workplace education on a regular basis by going to conferences, reading professional journals, and mentoring others. Increases in participation among virtually every group of adults surveyed underscore the unprecedented demand for adult learning.

Learning occurs through your work as well as through your experience in different jobs, with different peers and leaders. Much of what you needed to learn was driven by your employer. Now it is the time to rethink how you learn and to establish your own priorities for personal growth and development within the context of your ongoing work.

Your PC and the Internet

There are many excellent new learning devices that you can use on your personal computer. For example, Rosetta Stone offers self-paced courses to learn foreign languages. Computer Professor, which advertises on television, offers courses to help you learn computer applications. Employers, schools, and university extensions offer the use of such software or references to them. There are also online universities that you can access online.

Using the Internet, you are now able to access and organize information instantaneously from different media and sources. The Internet permits just-in-time learning—acquiring knowledge that you need to address an immediate need. For example, through webmd.com or similar websites, you can research a disease or illness, or even do a preliminary screen of possible causes of symptoms you are experiencing. If you are considering travel, you can research various travel websites. In researching information for this book, the authors found amazing access to research reports and studies that would have been difficult and costly to obtain years ago. Wikipedia, EB.com, and other websites replace old-fashioned encyclopedia volumes.

Amazon or Barnes and Noble, as well as local and university library online catalogues, make it easy to identify published books and other media that relate to a topic of interest.

Through the Internet, you can connect with people worlds away, grow social relationships, leverage information, and make interconnections through a diverse array networks and activities. Websites such as linkedin.com help you link up professionally with others who have common interests or who may help you out when you need them. Telephone books are replaced by easily accessible websites such as 411.com or whitepages.com. Maps and driving directions are available from sites such as mapquest.com and google.com (just enter your destination address).

Search engines such as Google have made it possible for you to research any topic and get pages of websites that may be helpful to you. Refined searches can help narrow down your choices to get the most useful ones. Every website seems to provide links to other websites, resulting in a trail of site hopping that can lead to very productive research results and exploratory learning.

To take full advantage of the resources on the web, you'll need to download software that plays media in different forms, especially video and audio files, pictures and graphics in various formats, and documents saved in the universal PDF format. Need help getting your computer skills up to par? Libraries, community centers, and schools typically have labs or classes to help you. Local computer consultants, computer stores, and even students from local schools are often eager to provide personal coaching on PC applications.

Formal Programs

Whether you are interested in a credit class, a certificate program, or a continuing education course, you can enroll at your local school, community college, or university. Extension and continuing education programs and online learning opportunities are relatively low-cost options. Many institutions offer reduced rates for retirees and adults over 55.

Consider the myriad of education venues that are readily available around the country offered through the following:

- Local adult schools
- University extensions
- Private vendors
- Parks and recreation
- Community centers
- Service clubs
- Professional organizations
- Places of worship
- Cultural centers
- Museums
- Specially funded institutes
- Topic-specific research and learning centers

Boomers are returning to campuses in growing numbers. Traditional-aged students are no longer the norm on college campuses and nontraditional age learners are expected to represent 50 percent of all enrollments by 2010. Estimates are that approximately one million people over age 55 enroll in college-delivered continuing and professional education courses, paying their own tuition for courses. Even greater numbers of adults engage in self-directed and non-formal education, looking to spend their increased longevity in new and productive ways.

Many companies offer employees tuition reimbursement for courses relating to their work or professional development. United Technologies Corporation pays full tuition and expenses for coursework leading to a degree and also provides matching time off. Upon completion of a degree, the employee also receives an award of company stock. You should take full advantage of company programs of this nature.

Sabbaticals

Talk with your employer about taking time away from work for an educational sabbatical so that you can enhance skills and proficiencies. More and more employers are viewing development as a retention strategy and are offering leave time to boomers and long-term employees. Consider asking your manager if you can "stop out" or take a break to renew your competencies with the intention of infusing new ideas into the workplace upon your return. Without incurring great financial sacrifice, sabbaticals may enable you to identify options that will expand your knowledge base and reestablish a sense of accomplishment. Surveys indicate that many companies offer paid or unpaid sabbaticals.

IBM offers employees with at least ten years of service an opportunity to study for a teaching career while remaining company employees. As part of a corporate commitment to reduce the shortage of science and math teachers, the company provided $15,000 in tuition to workers who wanted to transition into teaching. This model is but one example of an out-of-the-box alternative that may inspire you to propose a similar option to your employer.

Social Action Projects

Community, professional, and civic groups often bring people together to deal with specific problems or issues. Focused on improving life in their community or in the nation, many people work for the betterment of social structures, education, human rights, and the environment. If you are interested in grass roots movements, want to identify problems and develop solutions, or have skills and expertise to offer, community-based programs can be exciting ways to learn and grow while making a meaningful contribution.

Many boomers have found that involvement in a community organization or charity provides inherent learning opportunities. Employers, too, encourage such involvement because it allows individuals to gain experience through leadership roles, teamwork and project management, public speaking, research, and networking. Involvement in service clubs such as Rotary or Kiwanis gives professionals opportunities for leadership and service that continue after retirement.

Elderhostel

Founded in 1975, Elderhostel (www.elderhostel.org) is the world's largest education and educational travel organization, offering educational and experiential programs in 90 countries and 50 states. The nonprofit organization serves adults 55 and older, offering more than 8,000 different programs as well as accommodations and meals. Serving approximately 160,000 people worldwide each year, many boomer-aged adults are attending programs and also joining virtual communities that foster ongoing engagement with others as an extension of face-to-face meetings. Committed to conducting research on adult learners and trends in education, the organization provides cutting-edge programming for boomers who thrive on quality learning opportunities in residential settings.

Elderhostel research found that boomers prefer small groups, hands-on experiential learning, plenty of free time on your own, active and shorter programs, and accessible pricing. These results are a reminder that, as a boomer, you have significant sway in affecting the very nature of program offerings. The boomer generation has tremendous lobbying potential to influence packaging, delivery approaches, and pricing.

One-Day University

Award-winning professors from major universities such as Harvard, Princeton, Cornell, Yale, and other top-tier schools engage individuals in day-long programs. At the One-Day University (onedayu.com), for a single day, you can explore subjects you love or dabble in topics that fascinate you. There are no tests, entrance exams, or stressors—simply live classroom-based offerings taught by faculty from America's most prestigious schools. Started by the former director of the Learning Annex, the largest continuing education school in North America, the one-day approach acknowledges people's busy schedules and offers a way to engage in learning as frequently as you like without long-term commitments.

Live and Learn Arrangements

If you are looking for creative ways to learn and grow, a variety of unconventional live/learn opportunities exist. Some retirees choose to live on a cruise ship year round, availing themselves of ongoing workshops, seminars, social activities, and colleagueship without having to go very far. The Internet is replete with information about sites and providers who offer live and learn opportunities.

For those who prefer land-based venues, co-housing offers an alternative, affordable living arrangement. This type of intergenerational, communal living provides reasonably priced, supportive, social environments for individuals who are willing to share chores, cooking, driving, and common areas. On-site facilities often include common spaces such as a yoga studio, meditation center, library, and community room, all of which enable individuals to live and "age in place" while remaining vital, informed, and connected to others.

University-Linked Retirement Communities

Retirement villages associated with universities enable individuals to pursue interests they didn't have time to enjoy when working full-time. Today, more than 50 developments on or near university campuses offer lifestyles that enable older adults and retirees to avail themselves of intellectual stimulation and the benefits of campus-based activities. Opportunities run the gamut from living and teaching at the university to accessing lifelong learning opportunities through the university.

University-linked communities are as varied as the schools that gave rise to this innovative concept. Those at Penn State, University of Arizona, Yale, Stanford, and Duke enable residents to live close to a university, join classes, walk down the street to attend a concert, baseball game, or even teach classes. For healthy boomers who have the wherewithal to afford this lifestyle, these communities are a way to contribute to others, exercise your brain, and have fun! Simply check out your local university to see if they offer such an option. If you are willing to relocate, books are available that describe university-linked retirement communities nationwide; the Internet is also an excellent resource.

Your Preferred Learning Style

As you consider the array of learning opportunities available to you, be sure take into account the ways you prefer to get information, seek meaning, and build your knowledge. Individuals vary in how they effectively and efficiently absorb information. Whether you are aware of it or not, you have a preferred learning or cognitive style. Self-assessment tools help individuals reflect on their habits and preferences. More than 75 of them are available to you. The results help identify your characteristic mode of perceiving, thinking, and problem-solving.

When deciding whether to attend a class, learn through experimentation, read a book, or listen to a tape, getting in touch with how you learn best will enable you to leverage your strengths to advantage. The following sections discuss three basic alternatives.

Listening

Many individuals have a preference for "auditory learning," taking in meaning through spoken words or numbers. How comfortable are you when someone gives you directions orally as opposed to providing a map or written directions? For example, do you

- Remember things that are said?
- Prefer to get news from the radio or television instead of reading the newspaper?
- Often know the words to songs?
- Like to use voice mail to communicate?
- Have a knack for recalling ideas that you hear or jokes you were told?
- Read something aloud that you wrote to determine whether it makes sense?
- Get easily distracted if there is background noise?
- Like to listen to books on tape or a CD to learn a language?
- Prefer to think aloud and talk through ideas and alternatives?
- Use reflective language such as, "I hear what you said" or "That rings a bell" when talking to others?

If the answer to most of these questions is "yes," you most likely enjoy lectures and oral presentations. You may also prefer facilitators who ask questions, engage you in conversation, and promote dialogue. Or at times, you may decide to sit down with a CD or audiotape in order to listen and learn at your own pace in a self-directed manner. Instead of reading a book, you prefer an audio book. Unlike younger generation learners who are facile at multitasking and are not distracted easily, you may be among those who are put off by certain sounds that interfere with your concentration. As you think about how to capitalize on this preference, you might consider working with a partner so that you can talk through ideas together. At work, be sure

to attend meetings so that you can hear what's happening and be part
of discussions.

Visual Learning

Others prefer to learn through reading written materials, whether
text or numbers. You may be adept at observing body language,
demonstrations, and images. For example, do you

- Like to read?
- Find specific pages or passages in a book quite easily?
- Go online to get the news or read the paper each day?
- Find it easy to find errors when proofreading a document?
- Prefer to send emails or written memos instead of calling?
- Use and read maps, graphs, and charts well?
- Use visuals, charts, graphs, or pictorials to convey ideas or concepts?
- Use language patterns that reflect your style such as "I see what you mean" when conversing?
- Underline or highlight words on the printed page to help you remember key facts or information?
- Take notes on your notes?
- Keep a journal or log?
- Write down telephone and house numbers to remember them?
- Sequence problems?
- Make use of templates, compasses, and protractors?

If you think that you're a visual learner, read books and subscribe
to journals and professional publications to keep current, engaged,
and informed. If you want to take a class, choose a facilitator who dis-
tributes lots of handouts. Join a book club. If your employer offers
workshops or programs, ask trainers to give you supplemental reading
lists and bibliographies so that you can pursue subjects more deeply if
you want. Tapping your visual preferences can be as simple as creating your own flash cards when learning a language.

Learning by Doing

You may prefer learning through experimentation, trial and error, and hands-on engagement. This style of learning is called kinesthetic learning.

For example, do you

- Want to feel and touch things?
- Like to put things together?
- Utilize objects, props, or items you can manipulate to make your point?
- Sketch out diagrams or drawings?
- Enjoy opportunities to move around and actively engage?
- Have a facility for putting things together?

Younger generations grew up with videogames, a highly interactive and hands-on experience. As a result, they prefer to learn through programs that resemble video games. As a kinesthetic learner, you may find it difficult to sit still for protracted periods, preferring instead to be actively involved when learning. On-the-job training, trial and error, and experimentation may motivate you. Search for opportunities to learn that allow you to use your hands as well as your brain to make learning fun.

Learning is an active process. We learn by doing. Only knowledge that is used sticks in your mind.
—Dale Carnegie

Some individuals learn and work in structured ways. Learning from an instructor or supervisor, following directions carefully, or consulting with someone in charge before making decisions are preferences. Structured learning tends to be more prescriptive and organized. Other persons prefer a more flexible, independent approach to learning. You may want to be able to move use a variety of learning approaches and resources and have the latitude to decide what and how to learn. Some individuals try to mix the two approaches—drawing from structured education, but reworking the learning and supplementing it in personal ways.

The bottom line is that you should assess your style and choose learning settings, materials, and approaches as appropriate. As you develop, stretch yourself in new and different ways. Try a computer-based learning program. Go back to college for a formal classroom course. You may find that you like a variety of learning approaches. It's never too late to develop new ways to enhance lifelong learning.

Expanding Your Comfort Zone

To learn and grow and change, you need to challenge the behaviors that you are comfortable with. You need to expand your boundaries and embrace new ideas and approaches. We have all seen people (many older people, but also young people) get set in their ways and avoid trying things that are new or different. A manager who gets set in his ways is often simply doing what is comfortable and avoiding changes that are uncomfortable or threatening. An engineer, architect, or musician may fall into a pattern of design that is familiar, but repetitive. With maturity, many people tend to avoid risk, or try not to rock the boat. They are relying on their knowledge and experience rather than being open to new ideas and approaches. They have set mental boundaries that are difficult to break out of because of habit or strong beliefs.

However, age is not the critical factor in learning and adapting to change. The critical factor is adaptation of attitudes and behaviors. Successful persons (of all ages) step outside their comfort zone to achieve new goals and stretch their performance. Great artists and composers have often changed their styles and adopted or invented new styles. Exposure to new forms and ideas, visiting new places, working with new people and in new environments, and acquiring new knowledge and skills all help persons break through their self-imposed zones. Learning and developing is the lever for embracing new mindsets and new behaviors. For example, Dr. Judith Bardwick has written that employees are breaking free of their comfort zone in traditional career and work patterns—and are thriving when they act as free agents and shape their own work patterns.

I am always ready to learn, although I don't always like to be taught.

—Winston Churchill

Taking Charge of Your Growth and Learning

Because your employer may not provide the support you need to define and address your learning needs, you'll have to take the initiative for your continuing development. You need to identify your own development needs and priorities, shape your own development plans, apply for posted jobs, sign up for available programs and workshops, and initiate development conversations with mentors or coaches.

Your learning and growth is up to you. How do you plan to stay current and proficient? What self-planning or independent learning are you contemplating if your learning needs are not being met in the workplace? Formal as well as informal learning may be necessary for you to cope with rapid societal change, technological developments, new life skills requirements, and evolving lifestyles. Additionally, shifts in your thinking may lead you to develop new priorities and move in different directions than those you explored earlier in life. The following sections discuss some suggestions for shifting your thinking as well as some action steps for planning your learning path.

Adopt a Learning Mindset

Reflect on your purpose and outlook. If you have a yearning for learning, you'll find the time and the way to accomplish it. If you want to do meaningful work, you need to develop the necessary skills and knowledge. Your attitudes shape your behaviors. The choices are yours. Here are some tips:

- Be hopeful and optimistic. Form an image of how things could realistically be as you take positive steps to grow both personally and professionally.

- Develop a sense of your own capability, recognize your power, and leverage your strengths instead of focusing on deficits or losses.
- Get in touch with what motivates you, and explore the many opportunities and options available.
- Be confident in your ability to learn and grow; commit yourself to being a person who is open to new knowledge and ideas.

Clarify Your Purpose

You need to challenge yourself about your commitment to continued learning and growing. What is your intent? Are you seeking to stay current in your field? Do you want to broaden or deepen your expertise? Is learning a means to an end? Do you want to earn the credentials for advancement or to work in a new field (for example, teaching, nursing, real estate)? Or is learning an end unto itself? Self-reflection has the potential to become an integral part of your learning process as you make meaning of the past and plan for what's ahead. The search for purpose will help you redefine your identity and set priorities for work, leisure, and personal fulfillment.

Chart Your Path for Learning and Growth

Planning and implementing your own learning and growth is up to you. As you explore options, you will find that you need to assess your learning agility, energy level, retention, interest, and ability to comprehend information. Your needs and learning approaches are unique and you may need to manage your personal process of learning and growth. Finding growth opportunities that meet your needs will require time and attention so you can identify learner-centered programs that fit your unique requirements, goals, and objectives. Try out these techniques:

- Learn and develop in ways that are meaningful to you. Tailor your learning to your style, pace, and interests.
- Evaluate alternative learning opportunities and determine which are best suited to your needs and your interests.
- Develop a roadmap, however fluid, to chart a course from where you are to where you want to be.

- Be deliberate, choosing alternatives that meet your needs and desires.

- Define action steps that you can take on your own initiative.

Study as if you're going to live forever, live as if you are going to die tomorrow.

—Maria Mitchell

Shape Your Learning Environment

Education and training situations are often oriented toward younger participants. As a boomer, you may sometimes feel discomfort, fear embarrassment, or lack confidence when you are participating in a younger learning group. In these situations, you can adapt your learning style to that of the group or, if appropriate, suggest ways the learning environment can be adapted to your needs as an adult learner. You may want to consider these actions:

- Give preference to smaller learning groups/teams where you can ask questions and participate more actively.

- Give preference to programs that involve the use of case studies and role playing. Encourage leaders and designers to use such techniques to encourage active participation in learning.

- Ask for concrete, relevant examples. Ask for materials to be concrete, not theoretical or abstract, and don't hesitate to ask the leader how the information is relevant—how it applies.

- Refresh your skills at listening, note taking, and interpreting and retaining information. You may go back to basic tools that are helpful (memory aids, study habits, time management, and so on).

- If you have eyesight issues, ask for future materials to be provided in somewhat larger print. Ask for visuals to be clearly visible (not too much text). Ask for better lighting. You may want to sit up front in a room rather than in the back.

- Ask for clearer enunciation by speakers, fewer distractions (open doors or windows, other concurrent activities), and more frequent breaks (avoid long periods of sitting or standing).

To optimize learning, you should challenge your own thinking and ideas. Change something inside of you to see things in different ways. To truly change your point of view, you need to go through a process of questioning assumptions that influence the way you perceive, understand, and feel about the world.

Apply What You Learn

Try out new roles or behaviors. Integrate new ideas into your life based on conditions dictated by new perspectives. Suggestions include the following:

- Participate in professional meetings, and take advantage of tuition reimbursement and open enrollment in company in-house workshops.
- Learn from vendors and contractors, take sabbaticals, get coaching and feedback.
- Take on new assignments and experiences that will challenge and stimulate learning. Work on task forces and project teams in order to be engaged. Access job posting, e-learning, and so on.
- To win a different job or change employers, improve your resume writing, interviewing skills, and job search savvy in today's labor markets.
- Help design and conduct training for others. You often learn more by teaching than you do by being taught!
- Ask for help and feedback in applying knowledge and skills to actual work, including translation, reinforcement, recognition, and peer encouragement. Find a peer or a counselor who will help you think through your preferences and options, and guide you toward appropriate learning opportunities.

At least once each year take stock of what you have accomplished relative to your goals and recharge your learning strategy. Think of yourself as growing better, not growing older. If you've been learning and developing, then *you are.*

I've retired from one career, but now I'm getting into two new ones!
—Harvey Schwartz

7

Take Advantage of Opportunities

The change in the nation's demographic structure is not just a temporary phenomenon related to the large size of the baby-boom generation. Rather, if the U.S. fertility rate remains close to current levels and life expectancies continue to rise, as demographers generally expect, the U.S. population and workforce will continue to grow older, even after the baby-boom generation has passed from the scene.

—Ben Bernanke

Myth: Jobs Are Not Available for Boomers

If you decide you are interested in working, will jobs be available? The answer depends partly on what happens in the labor market, partly on the attitudes and policies of employers, but largely on your own attitudes and initiative. As a boomer professional, work will be available for you, if you sell your experience, knowledge, and skills effectively. Whether as an employee or as a free agent, the opportunities will be out there for you, but you will need to seize them.

Employers traditionally have expected boomers to wind down their careers and retire by age 62 or 65, rather than extending their working careers for five or ten more years as many boomers would like to do. Companies expect older workers to make way for younger talent to be developed and advanced into larger jobs. They seek to maintain an orderly flow and development of talent through their organizations and their decisions are sometimes influenced by age bias.

Ironically, some employers and economists are today worrying that too many boomers will retire in the decades ahead, leaving behind job vacancies that cannot be filled by qualified workers. They worry that specialized knowledge and experience will be lost as key individuals retire. They worry that the generations replacing the boomer generation will not be large enough or capable enough to meet future needs. The resulting workforce crisis, some believe, will impede company performance and slow economic growth.

> *Even with immigration, more women in the workforce, offshoring, the impact of technology, and extending the working lifetime all layered together, there still may not be enough people to get us there.*
> —Valerie Paganelli, Watson Wyatt consultant

However, there may be no crisis at all. Boomer managers and professional and technical workers may not retire early; they may stay in the workforce and simply be older. Regardless of changing economic conditions, the labor supply and demand marketplace tends to find a natural balance. If a demand for talent exists, boomers will be attracted to jobs that are unfilled, as will people from different occupations and qualified immigrants.

The demand for talent may be adjusted by redesigning work itself, better tailoring work to available talent, eliminating work through technology and productivity enhancements, or outsourcing work to regions or countries where talent is available. Balancing supply and demand may mean higher wages and more attractive terms and conditions for work. It also means the coming crisis will be worsened if we unduly restrict immigration of high-talent workers with the skills that are in short supply.

By 2010, the number of people ages 55–64 in the U.S. population will expand by 52%. If boomers leave the workforce as expected there may not be enough people to do the work. However, if a substantial number of boomers remain at work, such a crisis would be averted. Combined with the Gen X talent currently in the workforce and the

Gen Y talent that is moving into the workforce, boomer talent can bridge any transitional shortfalls.

Likely Work Opportunities

As a boomer professional, the aging of the workforce presents to you a great opportunity rather than a problem. The retirement of some boomers, combined with creation of new jobs in the economy, mean greater demand for your skills as a boomer professional. If a talent crisis develops for employers, you will have more opportunities to stay on at work or to shape jobs that match their needs with your skills and interests.

Even today, two in five men and three in ten women in America ages 55–64 who have pension income are also employed. A Government Accountability Office (GAO) study observed that potential skill gaps from impending retirements and a slowdown in the growth of the labor supply are likely to make older workers a resource of growing importance.

As discussed in Chapter 2, "Consider Flexible Work and Retirement," surveys indicate that boomers are more likely than the previous generation to remain in the workforce. As a boomer, you may choose to stay in your current career or move into a different line of work. You may stay with your current employer or join another in full-time, part-time, or free agent roles. Projecting such changes in workforce participation five or ten years into the future is difficult because boomers such as you will make decisions that will define future trends.

None of this is automatically obvious to employers. You and your colleagues should encourage employers to accept and adapt to a workforce that includes more persons in their fifties and sixties. You and your colleagues should press for more flexible work arrangements, customized pay and benefits, training and development, and other practices that will attract and retain older talent. As free agents (entrepreneurs, consultants, contractors), you'll need to work out arrangements that meet your needs as well as your clients'.

Few organizations are prepared for the repercussions of this exodus, both in terms of the experience and knowledge that will be leaving and the new population that will be entering.
—Miller and Katz

This chapter provides information and insights on the opportunities that these perceived talent shortages will create for you, as a valued professional, manager, or technical worker. You will learn about the boomer workforce and how the overall workforce will change if more boomers stay at work. This chapter also prompts you to think about whether your particular experience and skill sets will be in demand—and whether you have knowledge that organizations value and fear losing. You may consider the opportunities resulting from economic growth (new work) and the open labor market that characterizes our economy. Finally, you'll consider obstacles that you need to overcome and the key choices you can make.

The Enormity of the Boomer Generation

Concern about impending boomer retirements arises from the fact that the boomer generation is extraordinarily large in comparison with the generations before it and following it. The boomer generation is indeed the largest ever born in America, with 75.9 million births in the years 1946 through 1964. It was nearly 18% larger than the previous generation.

However, younger, subsequent generations are not as much smaller as many people think and therefore the talent shortage will not be severe. Generation X, following the boomers, the "baby bust" generation, is often cited as being 16% smaller. However, as noted in Table 7.1, Gen X is usually defined as embracing births between 1965 and 1976, or 12 years. If it is extended to match the 19 years of births included in the boomer generation, it is only 8% smaller. Gen X talent have been in the shadow of the boomers for a long time, waiting for boomers to make way. Gen Xers are likely to be well prepared to fill managerial, professional, and technical jobs as they are vacated by boomers.

Similarly, Generation Y, the "echo" generation or "millennial" generation (because it began entering the workforce at the turn of the twenty-first century), is larger than Gen X and is nearly the size of the boomer generation when the years of births are again expanded to be of comparable duration. This generation (ages 6–24 in 2008) has extraordinary talents, and many individuals are capable of accelerated development and larger assignments as boomers withdraw from the workforce.

TABLE 7.1   Current Generations in America

Birth Years°	Generation Name	Ages in 2008	Births (Million)
1928–1945 (1925–1945)	Silent	63–79	63.9
1946–1964	Baby Boom	44–62	75.9
1965–1983 (1965–1980)	Gen X	25–43	69.9
1984–2002 (1981–1999)	Gen Y Echo/Millennial	6–24	74.9

°Generation time frames are adjusted to be of similar duration. The time periods often defining these generations are indicated in parentheses.

The changes in the workforce, as in American culture, are slow to evolve. Generations are not distinct, with clear bright lines based on years of birth. In fact, many of the boomers born late in the generation have more in common with older Gen X members because of the social environment and experiences they grew up in (they were too young to remember Vietnam or the JFK assassination). Similarly, the line between Gen X and Gen Y is fuzzy. As discussed in Chapter 8, "Engage Younger Generations," these generations have much in common and differences are often exaggerated in importance. In her book, *Generation Me*, author Jean Twenge addresses characteristics of the baby boomers' children, born from 1970–2000, which blends Gen X and Y. It is good news that all three generations prominent in our workforce today can share common attitudes and values, value their differences, and thereby work together effectively.

Boomers Will Stay in the Workforce

Most of the studies that foresee labor shortages in the future assume that retirement patterns will be unchanged going forward; that is, that people will retire at the same age even as life expectancy and the ability to work longer go up.

—Peter Cappelli, The Wharton School

The workforce is made up of all persons who are working or looking for work. Past experience suggests that the 55 and older age group,
which has typically had lower participation rates than younger age
groups, will lower the overall labor force participation rate as it grows,
leading to a slowdown in the growth of the labor force. Further, as they
retire, the over-55 set will drive up health care costs and strain the fiscal strength of Social Security.

Actually, the U.S. workforce is projected to grow by nearly 15 million persons from 2004–2014, about 1% per year. This would be about
1.5 million or only .2% fewer people than during the 1994–2004
decade. The workforce won't shrink in the decade ahead; it simply
won't grow as rapidly as the economists believe is necessary to support
their targeted economic growth. The unemployment rate is expected
to slow down to 5.0 percent in 2014—0.5 percentage point lower than
in 2004.

Participation in the workforce varies with the life stages of the
population, as reflected in Table 7.2 and as follows:

- Young people, under age 25, are slow to enter the workforce because they are engaged in education. Their delaying working in
  order to gain education may be a good thing, yielding higher
  skilled, more valuable workers. Employers accordingly have a
  direct stake in the access to and quality of education in America.

- Persons age 25–54 are most likely to participate in the workforce. Women have entered the workforce in large numbers and
  their participation rate has leveled off to nearly that of men.
  However, there is a recent trend for fewer men to participate.

- Persons age 55 and over are likely to withdraw from work or
  work fewer hours.

TABLE 7.2   U.S. Workforce Participation Rates (%)

	1984	2004	2014
75+	4.3	6.1	9.6
65–74	15.3	21.9	26.9
55–64	51.2	62.3	65.2
25–54	81.8	82.7	85.4
15–25	67.7	61.1	59.1

Data Source: Toossi, 2005.

Bureau of Labor Statistics projections include a continuing gradual increase in labor participation by mature workforce (55 and older) based on past trends. However, because of factors addressed in this book, the participation rate will likely increase more than this, with the effect of retaining substantially more talent in the workforce. The increased participation rates will be higher due to better health, increased longevity, desire to stay at work, and the need for income and asset-building. Any increase in the retirement age of boomers will have a large effect on labor supply because the group is so large.

Compared with all other age groups of the labor force, the 55-years-and-older group has the most potential to increase its labor force participation rate further, and that may contribute to an increase in the growth of the labor force in the future.
—Toossi

Workforce participation by boomer women has been steadily increasing, a trend expected to continue in Gen X and Gen Y, although it will likely level off. After dramatic increases in the boomer generation and participation by women over four decades, the workforce today is comprised of 46% women and 54% men. In the next ten years, these percentages will shift to 47% women and 53% men. Among older workers, there is a trend for men to be more likely to leave the workforce. Among boomer professionals, we may expect women to stay at work longer—given their longevity, health, and the need for many to earn income and save for retirement. In many cases, they also began their careers at ages older than men.

A Permanent Change in the Workforce Age Mix

Even after all the baby boomers have exited the labor force, the increase in life expectancy and decrease in fertility rates will result in an aging of both the population and the labor force.
—Toossi

The net effects of the changing participation rates and the sizes of different workforce age groups will be profound. As shown Figure 7.1, by 2014, the workforce will have a much more evenly balanced representation by the different age groups than today.

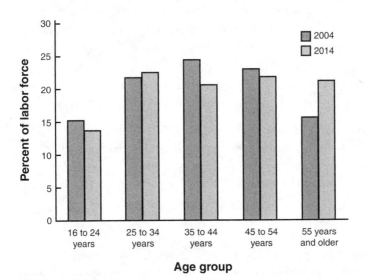

Figure 7.1   Workforce Distribution Projections by Age

Source: Bureau of Labor Statistics

The double effects of the larger number of persons who are older, plus the higher labor force participation rate among them will make over-55 workers a significant and permanent segment of the workforce. Workers over age 55 will no longer be perceived as those few who did not retire, but rather as a natural and expected part of the workforce.

As workers over age 55 remain in the workforce, they will become more visible, will leverage their skills and knowledge to stay at work, and will inevitably be working side by side with younger workers. The substantial number of older workers and the relative balanced size of the age groups will promote greater understanding and respect among workers of different ages. Organizations will ultimately adapt to age diversity, just as they adapt to gender and race diversity.

Managerial, Professional, and Technical Talent

Your opportunities to continue to work after age 55 are likely to be abundant if you are a boomer in a managerial, professional, or technical occupation. You are likely to have skills and knowledge that employers most want to retain, tap in creative ways, and develop further.

As boomers stay on at work, the quality of the workforce will be sustained and enhanced by the retention of older workers who are highly experienced and trained. This will be particularly important in industries and occupations that rely on critical professional skills and knowledge. In addition to their work, they will also facilitate transfer of this critical knowledge to others and mentor younger talent in their development.

Table 7.3 shows boomers' large share of our population and the scope of the challenge and opportunity to engage boomers in work rather than full retirement. In 2005, managerial, professional, and technical occupations included 19 million boomers, approximately 40% of the total in the U.S. workforce.

TABLE 7.3   Baby Boomer Generation Workforce Profile, 2005

	Age 16 and Over	Age 42 Through 59
Births		75,900,000
Population	226,082,000	72,809,000°
Civilian workforce	149,320,000	58,034,000°
Employed	141,730,000	56,000,000°
Managerial, professional, and technical occupations	49,245,000	19,432,000°

*Estimates based on information from BLS Reports, Employment Status of the Civilian Non-Institutional Population, 2005, and Employed Persons by Occupation, Sex, and Age, 2005.

The opportunities are driven not only by the need to replace retiring workers, but also by a gap between current labor demand and a projection based on new jobs required for economic growth. The needs will be greatest in two key groups: managers, who tend to be older and closer to retirement, and skilled workers in high-demand, high-tech jobs. Older boomer professionals are more likely than most workers to have pensions, personal savings, and other retirement assets, permitting them to choose to retire. However, they are also more likely to enjoy their work and spend their earned income.

Economists note that higher-income individuals, generally managers and professionals, may have more motivation to remain in the labor force, because their opportunity cost of retiring is greater than that of workers who earn a lower income.

Even though the Gen X "baby bust" cohort is smaller, the number of graduates from colleges and universities who are the new knowledge workers has continued to rise year after year. In fact, a larger share of Gen X workers are graduates because they had the opportunity to attend college. There were roughly 930,000 bachelor degree graduates per year in the 1970s when the peak of the baby boom was of college age. At the lowest point when the baby bust cohort was college age, there were 1,169,000 graduates per year. Peter Cappelli, a professor at The Wharton School, noted that Wharton did not cut back the size of its graduating class when the baby bust cohort came through. Neither did most institutions of higher education.

There are likely to be ample college graduates in most professional and technical occupations. Colleges today are going beyond traditional college age students, attracting many older persons who are returning to school to earn degrees or improve their skills, knowledge, and qualifications. Colleges and universities are becoming more attractive by becoming more accessible, with distance learning and more flexible programs.

To make the most of the opportunities available during this transition, you should seek out the specific occupations and specific industries where shortages are most likely to occur. Look for jobs that require skills and knowledge that match, or are close to, those that you have developed and mastered. When you were a young professional, you may have sought to be broad and flexible, so as to adapt to opportunities and/or progress into management in the long-term. As a boomer, you may prefer to develop a specific specialty that puts you in the highest demand classification.

Minimizing Knowledge Loss

Some organizations are concerned that they will lose specialized or proprietary knowledge when boomers walk out the door. Employers feel that critical human knowledge and capabilities are at risk of being lost in such areas as petroleum engineering, nuclear power plant operation, international trade, manufacturing processes, product design, and engineering. These fields require the development of talent over a long time, including knowledge, experience, and specialization.

Additionally, there is the risk of losing organizational knowledge as managers, project managers, and others retire without developing their successors. This includes knowledge of the social culture, the people (who knows what, who knows who), and how people collaborate and share knowledge to get things done. It also includes structural knowledge—the organization's processes, systems, and procedures—how decisions get made, resources get allocated, and results achieved.

The risk of knowledge loss may be exaggerated in many situations. Traditionally, employees have retired and taken their knowledge with them. This has always been a risk for employers. Yet employers have been encouraging older workers to leave through restructuring, early retirement incentives, and so on. This shows disregard for any special knowledge or skills they may have had that were lost when they left.

Companies are typically leaner than they once were and they lack the depth of talent to replace retirees immediately with qualified talent. Since the 1980s, many have paid less attention to preparing talent to fill vacated roles and to give them the working knowledge they need from those leaving. Companies used to have more flexibility and time to develop future talent. In those old days, some talent-deep organizations sought to have at least two ready backups for key positions and these high potentials were often themselves 40 or 50 years old.

Retention of knowledge is vital to sustain innovation, which most often builds on expertise, past experience, and learning. It is also vital to sustain the capacity for growth, to improve efficiency, and restrain costs. Overall, knowledge is a source of competitive advantage in an industry.

Almost two-thirds of respondents to a survey by Delong said that retirements in their organization will lead to a brain drain. However, the issue did not seem to be on the front burner, as studies revealed that fewer than one in four respondents said the issue is strategically very important for them today. Most organizations intend to deal with the looming wisdom withdrawal when the time comes that it is a pressing issue.

You may want to help your organization assess its risks and find solutions for knowledge retention. What can you do? Here are some suggestions:

- Discuss risks and solutions through informal discussions with colleagues or business line managers.
- Survey senior specialist line managers about knowledge areas that may be at risk.
- Survey or personally debrief employees when they terminate or retire.

You may also help enable knowledge retention in your organization, joining in an existing effort or starting one up:

- Foster informal knowledge-sharing networks in high-risk areas.
- Identify informal knowledge networks and use of web-based knowledge management tools.
- Establish formal knowledge management systems (web-based tools, inventories).
- Participate in or conduct training programs on knowledge sharing.
- Mentor and develop younger persons to help them engage in knowledge sharing.

As a boomer, you need not consider yourself to be competing with younger workers, but instead complementing them. The most effective way to retain and use the experience and wisdom you have developed is to stay and contribute, and over time, share your knowledge with others.

Effects of an Open-Labor Market

Occupations that face critical shortages include registered nurses and other health care professionals (for whom boomers will be increasing the demand for services), teachers, engineers, scientists, and technicians. Labor supply gaps may develop, but are filled by the natural and inevitable dynamics of the labor market. Supply expands to meet market demand, as long as it is an open market, qualifications requirements are adaptable, and wages rise. It may take a long time, but the supply and demand for talent will usually balance out. Talent is attracted to fields where jobs are available.

Peter Cappelli defines a labor shortage as essentially an employer's inability to fill jobs at prevailing wages. Shortages may be corrected if the will is there to attract talent. For example, he suggests that the prolonged shortage of nurses in America might be corrected through an upward adjustment in pay. However, health care employers have not had the resources or the will to make nursing pay sufficiently attractive to increase the supply. Other economists have also argued that the competitive market should be allowed to raise compensation rather than adopt policies that keep labor costs low.

It's tough to say there is an absolute talent shortage until there is full employment. The American economy has experienced low unemployment, but never full employment. And when unemployment falls, employers typically have to compete more aggressively for talent, by raising wages or otherwise making their jobs attractive. In the years ahead, we may expect close to full employment of talent in a certain few occupations. We can expect the market to adjust accordingly.

Employers can also attract talent from other occupations or geographic markets by making the jobs more attractive and/or increasing pay/wages. For example, companies needing IT talent drew from allied fields, such as engineering and mathematics. The accounting profession, facing chronic shortages of trained talent, has turned to recruiting graduates in liberal arts and other fields, focusing on their aptitude rather than their subject knowledge of accounting. Over a longer period, young people migrate toward occupations that represent the greatest opportunities. Educational institutions are typically slow in making changes in their enrollments or curricula to enable workers to move into a high-demand field, but ultimately the migration occurs.

When there are talent shortfalls, employers may also redefine the demand for talent by redesigning the work, adopting new technology, or outsourcing the work. Outsourcing the work to contractors shifts the worries and responsibilities to another business that makes it their focus. Information services firms (for example, IBM, EDS, CSC, and Accenture) build expertise, establish technical systems, and manage processes with costs that would be difficult and costly for a user company to match. Employees of the outsource vendor are "core" to the business, thus providing stronger identity and career opportunities.

Filling Some Needs Through Immigration

Immigrants, particularly in professional and technical occupations, have the potential to fill future gaps. As a result, such immigration is a benefit to our economy, not a threat. Talent has become a global market—and it moves to the economies where opportunities exist. Any shortages of critical skills may be eased in large measure by our willingness to welcome qualified talent from other countries.

Immigration is particularly important when we have shortages of specific professional or technical talent, relative to the jobs available. During the 1996–2000 periods, American high-tech businesses welcomed tens of thousands of workers with computer and software skills. Special H1B visas enabled businesses to bring in professional talent to work side by side with locally recruited talent. The flow slowed greatly when limits were set on the number of such visas and as the slowdown occurred in the high-tech sector after 2000. Another example is the great influx of nurses from other countries. A significant source of nursing talent has been the Philippines, seemingly to the point that we have prompted a shortage in that country.

There might be concern that such immigrants stay and become part of the permanent workforce, potentially contributing to higher unemployment when the economy has fewer jobs. However, the U.S. economy rarely, if ever, has a surplus of talent—particularly in managerial, professional, and technical fields. The economy has grown steadily for decades. The current talent shortages, as noted, are based on gaps relative to growth projections, not today's jobs.

Adding talent to our workforce on short notice is difficult. Companies have failed to ensure an adequate supply of trained talent, in part because of reduced investments in training and education in recent decades (when rightsizing took management priority). It also takes time for companies to shape and execute plans for recruiting and placing professionals into local jobs from overseas. To bridge the gap, it will be helpful for boomers to remain a few years in the workforce to fill needs (and pay taxes), but the longer-term future will depend in some part on immigration of workers of all kinds.

Taking Economic Growth into Account

Projections of labor requirements and possible shortages are based on assumptions of economic growth. The Federal Reserve Board projects that annual economic growth over the next decade will fall to less than 3%, down from 3.2% annual gains through the 1990s. Expectations of a slower growth rate are based on assumptions of slower economic activity in housing, less capital investment and productivity improvement through IT applications and process improvements, and slower growth in consumer spending. Business cycles themselves have a marked impact on the rate of economic growth. The federal budget, the demands of rising costs of federal entitlement spending (for example, Social Security and Medicare), the budget deficit, and growing annual costs of interest on debt, are among the factors that adversely affect economic growth.

Slower economic growth may not be such a bad thing, even though we have become accustomed to making the economic pie bigger and bigger. It does mean slower tax revenue growth. It also means fewer new job opportunities for American workers and ultimately lower standards of living in America. But it may also ease workforce shortages.

The essential fact is that changes in economic growth, reflecting business cycles, determine labor demand, not demographics and labor supply. It is the number of jobs, not the number of persons in the workforce that reflects and drives economic growth. The workforce includes both people with jobs and the unemployed. The workforce is highly adaptable and constrains economic growth only if the economy is at full or nearly full employment, and this is rare.

Economic growth also depends on productivity growth—expanding the overall product faster than the workforce. Capital investment, productivity improvements, and technological innovation have driven much of our productivity growth since the 1990s. This will continue, unless dampened by high oil prices, high interest rates, or other adverse factors.

Eliminating Obstacles for Boomers at Work

Employers often feel that there is a time for everyone to leave—to retire, to move on, to make way for younger folks. Age was once a convenient marker for the career cycle, including retirement timing (at age 62 or 65). Management succession plans and performance evaluations once included age as a defining factor. Mandatory retirement used to allow employers to say goodbye without regrets on either side.

However, times are changing. Discrimination in employment has been prohibited under the ADEA of 1967 and subsequent amendments. Mandatory retirement at any age was banned by federal law in 1986. Great progress has been made in eliminating race and sex discrimination, and age discrimination is fading away gradually. As long as there were few older persons in the workforce, there was little social pressure to change practices or attitudes.

A dynamic labor market gives more flexibility to boomers and to companies—to permit experienced talent to fill vacancies. But at the same time, an organization has the opportunity to be a more stable and attractive employer by minimizing the churning (loss and replacement) of its talent. When necessary, companies restructure and reduce the number of higher-paid jobs, many of which are held by older workers. Age discrimination may occur, but is not usually intentional.

Age distributions vary widely among companies—some are young, some have older profiles, typically reflecting peak hiring periods and retention. State Farm, IBM, and other large companies have actually brought their average ages down through aggressive changes in their organizations and workforces. Today's dynamic organizations shape plans with different staffing models to fit business needs in different segments of the business and workforce. Some segments have higher turnover, some have older, longer-term staff, and some have more contingent/short-term staff.

The baby boom has brought us a tremendous number of persons over age 50 who want to continue at work and who refuse to be treated as less capable or desirable than others or than they ever were. Boomers expect others to recognize that they still are energetic, creative, knowledgeable, productive, and otherwise capable of staying on at work and performing effectively. If they are not so recognized, they expect the opportunity to make their case, to persuade managers, and otherwise overcome obstacles that are not directly based on age, but are subtly so.

Even today, age bias begins to be apparent in organizations for employees between the ages of 50 and 60. A survey of 294 senior executives by the Association of Executive Search Consultants found that age discrimination begins to be apparent as early as age 40, as shown in Table 7.4.

TABLE 7.4   Percentage of Executives Reporting Age Discrimination

Age 40 or 45	19.4%
Age 50 or 55	61.1%
Age 60 or 65	12.0%
No age discrimination	7.5%

Source: *Wall Street Journal Online*, 2006.

If boomers want to continue to work instead of retiring abruptly, they will need to overcome the obstacles of biased attitudes and employer practices. Boomers will survive longer, be in better health, will stay active, and will make their presence known.

Cultural stereotypes, often reflected in fashion and media, are slow to change. American culture is still youth-oriented. Television producers target the age 18–35 demographic group. Ironically, while there are widely held stereotypes of older persons, there is typically no such bias against individuals who are known well and respected by coworkers on a personal basis. As with other forms of prejudice, attitudes become more positive as people get to know members of the other group better. Encouraging interaction among generations helps reduce ageism.

The age of persons is becoming more difficult to judge by their appearance and behaviors. Boomers have adopted all sorts of means to appear younger—by physical appearance, dress, behavior, interests, or fudging their resumes. This does not reduce bias, but merely avoids it. We believe boomers should demonstrate that age simply isn't relevant. As a boomer professional, you need to show that you have what it takes and that you expect to be treated with the respect and fairness that you deserve.

The following bolded sentences are persistent attitudes toward older workers that have an adverse impact on their opportunities at work, accompanied by suggestions for you to overcome these obstacles.

"Boomers don't have current skills and knowledge." When professional workers retired in the previous generation, few pursued work after abrupt retirement because of their lack of portable skills. As their careers evolved within a company, most became qualified only for specific, specialized jobs. Others were the prototypical managers in gray flannel suits who "knew the organization" and whose skill sets were often job or company specific. Most boomer professionals have developed more portable skill portfolios. Most remember reading *What Color Is Your Parachute?* (Bolles, 1972), which promoted self-analysis, skill development, and self-reliance in career planning. Boomers have typically continued to develop and use their talents, believing that career planning and development is key to success—and many enjoy support from their organizations. As a boomer professional, you should develop an adaptable portfolio of skills and knowledge as your critical asset in finding the work you desire.

It may be that older workers were educated long ago, but this does not mean that they are out of date. Further, they do not necessarily have difficulty learning new technology applications and other practices. As a boomer professional, you should, of course, pursue continual learning to keep your skills and knowledge fresh and in tune with demands. Education, company training, certifications, and personal learning all are available to professional employees. Focus on the specific knowledge and experience that are most relevant to the work you want to pursue. You need to emphasize your current expertise in your resume, your conversations, and at every other opportunity.

"Boomers are less flexible, less capable of change, and favor the status quo more than younger persons." A common attitude is that boomers don't fit the more contemporary, informal, and networked organizational culture, and they are the first to object to new ideas and the last to get on board when the organization adopts them. As a boomer professional, do you take offense to this? Rigidity and resistance occurs among workers of all ages but is least likely to be characteristic of boomer professionals who are eager to stay active in work, knowing full well of the changes occurring around them and expected in the future. Show that you are a supporter, enabler, or leader of change—emphasize your experience and accomplishments. Show your understanding of issues that call for action and your eagerness to improve the current situation.

"Boomers are less creative and innovative." Some organizations seem to have a "Dracula complex." According to attorney Jonathan A. Segal, "They want newer and fresher blood, because they're under the mistaken impression that it can bring vitality to an organization. However, experience and research show us that vitality, productivity, and creativity are not age-related at all." As a boomer, you need to present your strengths in being creative and innovative. Your own style may suggest that you are better at day-to-day incremental innovation rather than out-of-the-box breakthrough innovations. Organizations need both.

"Older workers don't relate well to younger generations in the workforce." Similarly, they are perceived less likely to work effectively in teams than younger workers. Actually, the contrary may often be true. Boomer professionals are less likely to be concerned with competition for career advancement and hence are prone toward collaboration. High-performing boomers work comfortably with people having different behaviors and styles. One study showed that younger workers preferred to work for an older manager; boomers indicated they didn't care whether their managers were younger or older. As a boomer professional, you should eagerly work with next generation talent. Collaboration is vital.

"Older workers act more slowly and do not share a sense of urgency." Older persons are suspected of "retiring on the job," letting others work harder to get the work done. This is also uncommon.

In well-managed organizations where there is a line of sight (empowerment, accountability), reinforced by rewards and performance management, professionals of all ages are expected to get the job done in a timely and quality manner. Where there are differences, the patience that some older persons may have helps balance the more impulsive tendencies of some younger persons. As a boomer professional, you can demonstrate that you can sense the pace and rhythm of an organization and you are committed to helping achieve objectives on a timely basis. You will carry your weight.

"Older workers are more likely to dominate senior positions." As a result, they are seen as blocking opportunities for development and advancement of younger talent (representing a "gray ceiling"). Yet few organizations today hire at the entry level and manage a flow of talent through the organization's levels. Instead, most hire talent at all levels, increasingly experienced talent—and there is an age mix at all levels (age diversity is a good thing). Senior assignments and tenure in them should be based on demonstrated skills, experience, and performance—not on age. As a boomer professional, you should identify clearly what senior positions require and emphasize your bona fide qualifications and demonstrated performance. Don't let your age be an issue.

"Older workers tend to be more expensive than younger workers, by virtue of their experience, tenure, and level." Older job candidates are seen as too qualified for the positions available, making them (supposedly) more costly and prone to boredom or disruption to the organization. In some firms, "maturity curves" have been used to pay engineering talent, paying individuals based on tenure and age, with the assumption that learning and skills increased early in their careers. Today, professional and managerial jobs are typically paid based on the value of the job (the work performed, level, impact, and so on), as well as the market value of the individual's talents (competitive pay for experience, qualifications, and so on). Hence in a well-managed organization, there should not be excessive pay given to older professionals and managers, but assignments and compensation should reflect the value that individuals provide. As a boomer professional, you should encourage managers to pay fairly—age itself is not a reason to get compensated more or less.

"They need more health care benefits and services, driving up health care costs." All individuals who have accidents, become ill, or suffer chronic conditions also incur extraordinary costs. The key idea of group insurance coverage is the pooling of cost risk to make sure everyone is covered. Excluding older workers as a class is hardly a thoughtful response. Government regulations permit employers to provide health benefits based on a common dollar value to all employees, even though this puts a burden on the individuals of any age who have extraordinary needs. As a boomer professional, look after your health care insurance needs—and, if you can, stay well, healthy, and fit!

Challenging Age Bias

It comes down to being between 30 and 35, you're fine, no problem. If you are younger than that you have to work hard to prove yourself. If you are older than that you have to work hard to convince people you still have what it takes. Everyone has to learn new things because new technologies come out every six months.

—P. Anderson

Surveys by Skladany and Sumser indicate that 65–70% of workers age 50 and over experience damaging age bias in their organizations. Employers indicate that they feel such opinions are exaggerated. Business and employer groups say there is no significant age bias anymore and that most employers act in compliance with laws. Yet older workers believe they are unfairly treated relative to younger workers. One study found concerns in these areas:

- Laying off employees: 58%

- Making hiring decisions: 44%

- Determining salary increases: 32%

- Promoting someone to a more responsible job: 25%

- Assigning desirable work: 23%

Another survey, conducted by Reynolds, asked 1,207 technology employees whether they had experienced workplace setbacks—layoffs, being passed over for promotions, missing out on bonuses, and so on. Of those responding, 40% said that age discrimination is a significant or widespread problem in the technology professions. However, another 40% disagreed. Techies younger than 35 were twice as likely as those over 45 to dismiss the age issue as insignificant. The study also noted that age discrimination sometimes also cuts the other way when young techies complained that they are perceived as too young and inexperienced.

If you feel you are unfairly treated, even with all of your own best efforts to remove your age as a consideration, you have the legal right to protest discriminatory actions under state or federal laws. In fact, it has never been easier for an individual to initiate a complaint process. In practical terms, however, personal influence may be more effective in opening up opportunities.

It is typically difficult to prove that adverse actions were age-related and intentionally so. ADEA and state statutes have not significantly reduced age bias and discrimination. Most EEOC complaints are resolved in favor of employers, as age discrimination is difficult to prove (60% are found to have no reason to believe that discrimination occurred). In many cases, individuals who filed did not provide satisfactory evidence to support formal charges. Only 10% of ADEA charges result in any kind of benefit being paid to the individual complaint. As a result, age discrimination is assumed to be under-reported. Many aggrieved workers never file charges and simply move on in their lives.

> We all aspire to live to be old and consequently we all must work to create a society where old age is respected, if not honored, and where persons who have reached old age are not marginalized.

—Richard Butler

Maximizing Your Opportunities

As a boomer, you need to allay fears an employer may have about older workers by showing energy, flexibility, reasonable pay expectations, up-to-date skills and qualifications, and a reasonable explanation of why you decided to change jobs or careers. Here are some suggestions:

- Expect fair, unbiased consideration. Expect proper, uniform job interview questions, without any relating to age. Expect consistency of all hiring and promotions decisions regardless of age. If you experience difficulties, look for employers that state that they value diversity.

- Simplify your resume. Shift your emphasis to your *value*, not your age and the many jobs you've held. Don't list every single job you've ever had, and emphasize your major accomplishments, not the years you spent in various jobs.

- Keep your skills and qualifications current relative to those valued in your field. Highlight specialty skills, technological proficiencies, and recent training that reflect enhanced levels of competence. Use contemporary, rather than outmoded language, to describe your experience, your accomplishments, and your interests.

- Keep a good relationship with your manager and colleagues at work so you'll know what is going on and you can comfortably talk with them about your interests and concerns.

- Think of yourself as a member of a skill group rather than part of an age group. Emphasize the need of an organization to have diversity of ages and experience to facilitate performance.

- Make a strong case for why someone should hire you. Describe your characteristics that are important to a hiring manager. Differentiate yourself from others based on the unique qualities, work ethic, and commitment you bring to the workplace.

- Keep a log of all occurrences you think might be construed as age bias. Also save emails, memos, and other documents as support for your claims, if they become necessary to support a complaint.

The potential shortages of managerial, professional, and technical talent present opportunities for you as a boomer. Whether you take advantage of the opportunities depends on your choices as you pursue your career. Here are some things to consider:

- Understand how the market is changing, what skills are in demand, what the future trends and emerging opportunities are, and how you might fit in. This calls for you to be market savvy—

networking, listening, and learning about shifts in jobs, talent movement, job opportunities, and the "best" employers.

- Understand the important skill, knowledge, and experience requirements and match your talents with them. Focus your attention on opportunities that look like they are a good fit. Make the most of your strengths—your knowledge and experience that are relevant—and translate your experience into value that is relevant to the opportunity.

- Figure out your strategy for working. Consider your options and focus on your preferred working arrangements: Stay in your current job? Redefine your job? Move to a different job—in the company or another? Or be a free agent, as a consultant or contractor?

8

Engage Younger Generations

We need to remember across generations that there is as much to learn as there is to teach.

—Gloria Steinem

Myth: Boomers Must Compete with Younger Generations in the Workplace

Do you remember the generation gap? Back in the 1960s, baby boomers began behaving in ways that departed significantly from how their parents and previous generations behaved. Many boomers were enthusiastic about rock and soul music, fast food, fashion, drug use, politics, and the sexual revolution. Parents generally disapproved of signs of their rebellious behavior—long hair, rock music, and protests. The gap was like a divide, and it resulted in serious generational conflicts. Some youths adopted a "hippie culture," and for many, Woodstock defined the generation.

Every generation has distinctive characteristics, shaped by the events and experiences of its members. As a boomer, you are aware that you share a common identity with your generational peers because of the common experiences you had. You also share values and viewpoints that are distinct from other generations. As Morris Massey said, "What you are is where you were when."

Boomer youth grew up in a post-war period of economic growth, optimism, and general affluence. Their world was in sharp contrast to the previous era, which included the Great Depression and World War II. Values and culture gaps between boomers and previous generations were accentuated by the large size of the boomer population.

The youth culture they created and their focus on remaining youthful has carried over to successive generations. Active and engaged, today's baby boomers do not want to be seen as old or obsolete. Given all the changes the boomer generation wrought, it is ironic that they are the ones on the defensive, sometimes viewed by younger individuals as being outmoded or lagging behind. Many now have to deal with perceived differences and resulting conflicts with younger generations that are creating a new generation gap.

In this chapter, we use the generic descriptors *boomer*, *Gen X*, and *Gen Y* to elaborate on the overarching characteristics of three key generations currently in the workforce, each of which possesses unique characteristics. Our aim is to help you understand the characteristics of other generations as well as your own and also to understand more fully the attitudes and behaviors of younger persons.

It is a myth that boomers must compete with younger workers for jobs and opportunities and that they will lose in this competition. Most of you will retain your capabilities as you grow older and have the added benefit of experience. While generational differences exist, they need not be source of conflicts among age groups. In reality, untapped potential exists for different generations to appreciate one another's strengths, communicate effectively, and work together collegially. As a boomer, you have an opportunity to collaborate with and influence the youth culture by bringing your talents, organizational insights, and wisdom to bear. Boomer professionals need to find ways to share expertise and insights with younger persons, learn from them to improve their own technology skills, and work effectively across generations to achieve shared objectives.

This chapter provides you with insights into why individuals from different generations click or clash. You'll understand the richness of the experience and behaviors of each generation and discover how capitalizing on generational differences can be a source of strength and competitive advantage.

Multiple Generations at Work

Differences among boomers, Gen X, and Gen Y individuals become evident when members of these respective generations work and learn together. However, in the long run, all generations want many of the same things. In Maslow's Hierarchy of Human Needs, safety, security, employment, and resources are baseline requirements that all people seek to satisfy. Additionally, higher order needs, such as friendship, respect, trust, recognition, and opportunities to learn and grow are examples of psychological and growth needs that people value regardless of their generation.

Some of the differences you encounter in your personal and professional life reflect people's different life stages such as childhood, adolescence, maturity, and late adulthood. Kids act like kids, in every generation, and what may seem rebellious in one generation occurred at a similar age period for others. *New York Times* writer, Virginia Heffernan, suggested that each generation has the tendency to accentuate its own distinctive experiences, not thinking that others before or others who follow may have similar experiences but in different social contexts. She argued that boomers make way too much of the unique greatness of their generation.

> *To say that you were born in 1946 to a world of hope, only to have innocence dashed in November 1963, and go on to discover sex and free thought in the subsequent years, is to say that you were born, turned 17, and grew up. It's not to contribute to the writing of a nation's history.*

—Virginia Heffernan

Leveraging Generational Differences

The mix of talent, experience, and viewpoints among different generations is simply another aspect of workforce diversity you can leverage. Not only will benefits accrue, but your life at work will be more pleasant. As Mark Twain suggested, "It is best that we should not all think alike; it is difference of opinion that makes a horse race."

As a boomer, you can engage individuals with attitudes and behaviors that differ from yours. You can help shape a work environment to accommodate generational differences and also capitalize on commonalities. For example, you may already be a cross-generational boundary spanner, communicating via email and instant messaging, problem-solving through teams and networks, implementing flexible work arrangements to accommodate varied needs, and designing training to meet unique learning styles.

> *Despite the prevalence of intergenerational workforces in every workplace, generational conflict is not widespread. Instead, organizations are reaping the benefits of the diversity provided by workers of different generations. Workers from different generations work effectively together and learn from one another. The most frequently reported problems are relatively minor and tend to stem from issues such as differing expectations regarding work hours and acceptable dress.*

—Society for Human Resources Management

By necessity, employers are seeking ways to motivate multiple generations at work and implement effective, cross-generation work practices. Partners at Deloitte designed and implemented innovative management approaches as part of a "Next Generation Initiative" to attract, retain, and engage Gen X and Gen Y professionals in tax, audit, and consulting careers. With two experienced workers leaving the workforce for every one inexperienced worker entering, boomers are a valuable resource for developing Gen X and Gen Y talent. An added incentive for employers is the avoidance of costs relating to recruiting and retaining talent, given that the cost of losing an employee is 1.5 times a person's salary. According to Sachs, the astounding estimate of $400,000—the amount of money it takes to replace an attorney—is prompting law firms to rethink their workplace policies. Many of today's newly minted attorneys are less concerned about becoming partners and more interested in work-life balance, flexibility, and opportunities to do philanthropic work.

In order to lobby employers to implement boomer-friendly workplace practices that are important to you, the first step is to identify your needs and determine how you can be a competitive advantage to an employer. Getting in touch with your own valuable traits, while also understanding the unique profiles of younger generation workers, will be a critical success factor in ensuring teamwork and collaboration in today's workplace.

Generations Are Defined by Shared Experiences

In ancient times, a generation was viewed as the period it took for a mother to replace herself with a grown daughter, about 30 years; hence, there were about three generations in a century. Today if a generation is defined by experiences shared in common, they can be much shorter—as little as 15–20 years. Social scientists remind us that public crises, wars, and trends often make fixing exact dates for a generation difficult. This means that generations come and go in relation to significant emotional events, critical incidents, and social moments in history. At some point, one generation fades away and another arises. And as noted demographers Strauss and Howe suggest, just as history defines generations, generations also define history.

By naming and noting observable behaviors, attitudes, and beliefs of different generations, you can uncover the origins of people's unique qualities and figure out how to tap into individuals' strengths. Coming to appreciate and accept generational characteristics that differ from your own can go a long way to opening communication channels and increasing trust with others. Your focus should not be on how to change other people to conform to your standards or values; instead, your goal should be to learn how to accept and understand people, acknowledging the validity of who they are.

We examine the differences and commonalities among the three primary generations in the workplace today (boomer, X, and Y) in this chapter. Most members of the "silent" generation preceding boomers have left the workforce. When you read about baby boomers, you may feel that some attributes of the generation apply to you, and other attributes do not. Not all characteristics apply to everyone. It may also be that you are a "cusper"—someone who is on the leading or trailing edge of one generation or another. Many later boomers feel they are more like younger Gen Xers. Generational lines are not crisp and bright. The boomer generation tends to be described in two groups: Woodstockers, first-wave boomers born mid-1940–1950, and second-wave, or young or shadow boomers, born 1950–1960 (see Table 8.1).

TABLE 8.1   Generational Identities

Generation Descriptor	Birth Years	Other Descriptive Names
Silent	1925–1945	Traditionalist, Schwarzkopf, GI, Veteran
Boomer	1946–1964	Woodstock, Generation Jones, Sandwich
Gen X	1965–1980	MTV, Boomerang, Twenty-Something, Baby Buster
Gen Y	1981–1999	Millennial; Echo Boom: Gen Next; Internet

Generational identity is typically shaped by a small part of an over-all generation, typically the members who went to college. For exam-ple, not all baby boomers were political radicals or liberals. In fact, one-third of early boomers served in Vietnam, and younger boomer voters were more likely to support conservative candidates. The boomers most commonly described are white collar, well-to-do pro-fessionals from middle to upper-middle class families. Data from a Duke University study (Campbell, 2005) highlights the divide that ex-ists between boomer "haves" and "have nots," reinforcing the reality that boomers' experiences not only differ from previous generations, but also from those of each other. There may even be greater differ-ences among boomers than among generations.

We must be careful not to apply generational characteristics to all members. The boomer generation is extremely diverse. There are eth-nic classes in the boomer generation who find themselves no better off than their parents despite efforts during the Civil Rights era. Accord-ing to the Population Reference Bureau (Hughes and O'Rand, 2004), "At midlife, boomers have the highest wage inequality of any genera-tion. Late boomers have the highest poverty since the generation born before World War I. Research reveals that at middle age, one in 20 boomers lives in poverty." Studies by Roper Starch Worldwide found approximately one-quarter of boomers are ill-prepared for retirement, with one in four saying that they do not expect to be able to retire.

Early Influences Define Generations

Most likely your attitudes, beliefs, values, and behaviors were formed during your formative years when you were between age 17 and 25—the height of your social and political awareness. This is because birth and coming of age are defining periods in people's lives that shape their generational personality. Individuals who grow up at the same time in history are influenced by factors such as the economy, societal attitudes, gender roles, and technology. Thus, generational cohorts are people born within the same period of years who share significant life experiences, historical events, and similar problems. Individuals on the same general life path tend to have the same ideas and share common norms. Just look around and you'll see how music, books, films and video, superstars, and heroes of the day influence the world views of successive generations.

To understand behavior at any stage in individuals' lives, we look to the stories people tell and the experiences they recount. Distinctive stories underscore the profound power of significant events in shaping the personalities of different age groups. People's descriptions of their common experiences offer insight into the origins of shared beliefs and help to explain the attitudes generational cohorts have towards the world and others.

Within a generation, individuals display different behaviors and interests. In fact, many of the characteristics attributed to boomers came primarily from college students, often white and middle class. Yet there were many boomers who were not in college, but were instead working or serving in the military. They were not protesting on campuses.

Consider September 11 and how the tragedy affected people differently based on their age and the centrality of the event to their phase in life. For the teenager who never experienced terrorism on American soil, it may prove to be a life-altering event. For the 55-year-old mother who lost her firefighter son, the experience sits on the shoulders of earlier life experiences and creates deeper, accumulated levels of meaning. And for the veteran who fought in WWII or Vietnam, this cataclysmic moment becomes entwined with other inextricable memories of war. Based on their ages, location at this fixed point in history, and significance and effect of this event, individuals may exhibit dramatically different behaviors and attitudes about family, risk-taking, trust, tolerance, and the future. They retain the memory of 9-11, impressions of which will continue to be influential throughout their lives.

Like the distinctive rings reflected in horizontal slices of California's giant redwood trees, historical events leave an indelible imprint on the personalities of distinctive generations. As you read the prototypical characteristics of boomers, Gen X and Gen Y individuals that follow, note that the descriptions are composite sketches that may or may not match your individual experiences or circumstances. We offer them as a vehicle to enhance your understanding of what influenced the identity of each generation and to appreciate generational differences in their own right.

The Boomer Generation

Within a year of the end of WWII, the demographic profile of America changed dramatically. Men and women who had experienced economic hardships and sacrifices of war became parents. Between 1946 and 1964, 92% of all women of childbearing age had children. Every eight seconds a baby was born—10,000 babies a day, two million a year—for 18 years. The resulting 76 million boomer babies, along with two million new immigrants in the same age group, changed society. Currently, each day an adult turns 60 every eight seconds in this country.

Boomers, agents of changes shaping the world today as they age, were raised by child-focused parents. Mothers and fathers, guided by the popularized philosophy of Dr. Benjamin Spock, honored permissive childhood development practices that influenced the behaviors the entire generation. Born into nuclear families with an average 3.8 children, boomer youth were raised to believe they could do better than their parents. Children were programmed from birth to abide by certain basic rules, envision a promising future, and aspire to be successful. Economic expansion eased the glide path for most boomer children to grow up feeling optimistic and positive. Given the time, money, and energy that parents invested in their offspring, boomers' childhoods were relatively trouble-free and contributed to the "can do" attitude that is still evident today among members of this cohort.

> *Blessed with great expectations of affluence and education, the boom children were raised as a generation of idealism and hope. War babies, Spock babies, Sputnik generation, Pepsi generation, Rock generation, Now generation, Love generation, Woodstock generation, Vietnam generation, Protest generation, Me generation. The names did not stick because the baby boom generation is a moving target. At every age it takes on a different character and presents us with a different set of problems.*
>
> —Landon Y. Jones

Boomer youth were seen as the hope for the future. Think about what it meant for you, as a boomer in 1967, to see *Time Magazine's* award for "Man of the Year" go to your generation. Consider the burden of proof such attention placed on individuals who people believed would champion causes and cure the world's ills. Although this was an awesome vision, many rose to the occasion believing that they would accomplish great things. Children reaped the benefit of having well-qualified teachers. Boy Scouts and Girl Scouts, learning to be good citizens, took pride in America's accomplishments as Sputnik instantiated the United States as a superpower.

Baby boomers were the first generation to grow up watching the 39.5 million televisions that graced America's living rooms. People watched the same shows, like *Father Knows Best, Ozzie and Harriet,* and *Leave it to Beaver*—idealized versions of life in suburbia where there was always a happy ending. Socialized by similar media, messages, and songs, generational members listened to rock and roll and Motown. Remember Elvis, poodle skirts, pop-it beads, hula hoops, the Beach Boys, and the Rolling Stones?

Yet at the peak of their awareness, and during a time when the economy was thriving, many boomers did an about face. Although conformity had been part of a way of life in the 1960s, when individuals scrutinized the world more closely, injustices and contradictions stood out. Serious issues of the day such as human rights and civil liberties grew out of a shared moral sense that inspired many to shift their attention to particular causes. Although privy to the benefits of economic growth, many individuals spent their late adolescence searching for deeper meaning. Despite the spirit of optimism that Kennedy engendered across the nation and a spirit of volunteerism evidenced in increasing Peace Corps enrollments, some boomers transitioned from a world of idealism to an age of discovery. Many explored spirituality and experimented with drugs, meditation, and alternative lifestyle choices. Intervention by the United States in Southeast Asia marked a significant turning point in history. Large numbers of draft-age boomers went off to fight, while others challenged the government's direction and struggled with their positions on the Vietnam War. Student protests made headlines as individuals rallied around issues of free speech and civil rights. "Hell no, we won't go" was the mantra for those opposed to the war.

For older boomers, permissive sexual behavior, drugs, and rising unemployment fostered a desire to experiment with new lifestyles; however, this was not the case for younger individuals born in the second, ten-year period of the boomer generation. For generational researchers such as Strauss and Howe, younger boomers were deemed to be "observers" of past events and unique moments in history; many did not actively participate in free love, protest movements, or the war as did their older generational peers. In their later years, first-wave boomers tended to be more interested in financial gain and the promise of American business, while second-wave boomers recognized the downside of blind faith in organizations and government. More skeptical about being able to trust institutions, younger boomers were interested instead in co-parenting and engaging with their children.

Kennedy's assassination was a seminal moment for all boomers. Most can recall exactly where they were when learning of his death. Similarly, the entire boomer generation shared significant life experiences and events in history: the Cuban Missile Crisis, assassinations of John F. Kennedy and Martin Luther King, Rosa Parks, passage of the Civil Rights Act, Kent State, women's liberation, the Persian Gulf War, and Watergate. All were all historical occurrences that shaped the boomer personality, prompting many to champion civil rights, rights of the handicapped, and privacy rights. While taking pride in the way they were transforming, boomers' anti-authoritarian attitudes were often manifested in the adage, "Don't trust anyone over 30."

In addition to being champions of others' causes, boomers also fought for opportunities for themselves. Although younger boomers often railed at the conspicuous consumption of Yuppies (young urban professionals) who were part of their generation, boomers generally were on the same path. Working hard to get ahead, individuals competed for power and position. Characteristically high achievers, boomers built stellar careers, attained managerial and executive positions, and demonstrated their competitiveness in a variety of arenas. They wanted visible recognition such as title, money, and perquisites to distinguish themselves from others. At the same time, many were concerned about having work that was meaningful and doing something that made a difference. Unlike their parents who often viewed work as an obligation, boomers wanted their work and workplace to be fun, more flexible, and engaging. Like many of today's Gen X and Gen Y individuals, boomers changed jobs and created new ways of working if they didn't like what was happening. A willingness to change characterized boomers' approach at work and resulted in their bringing innovation and flexibility to the workplace. As more and more boomer women and super-moms entered the labor force, more humane and equitable work environments emerged.

Despite making professional strides, many boomers experienced strained marriages and ultimately divorced. In 1975, the number of divorces passed one million for the first time; at the end of the decade, the U.S. had two times as many divorced people. Cultural norms suggested it was acceptable to leave a marriage if things were not working and, ironically, contributed to more egalitarian childrearing practices as men assumed active parenting roles.

Today, boomer men and women are successful in both profit and non-profit sectors. Boomers pay 60% of all taxes in the country and have the highest volunteerism and contribution rates of any generation. This self-empowered generation also has a history of embracing teamwork. Many boomers led important business innovations, popularizing employee empowerment and involvement, team-building, participatory leadership, and flat and matrix organizational structures. As a member of this generation, you boast a rich history of self-improvement and having high expectations of other people. In fact, your generation is known for thriving on competition. At times boomers can be judgmental, expecting coworkers to perform as they do. No doubt at some point you were called a "workaholic" as boomers are well known for struggling to strike a balance between work and play due to a strong work ethic.

> *Work has held a singular importance in their lives. Their fathers had proved themselves worthy in World War II— tempered by war, disciplined by a hard and bitter peace. The Baby Boomers—most of them—would have to be tested on the job. Business would be their war, the competitor their enemy. They would win or lose their personal battles on the warship called "work." They've tended to define themselves through their jobs and to achieve their identity by the work they perform. For this generation, "work ethic" and "worth ethic" are synonyms.*

—Zemke, Raines, and Filipczak

Individual differences notwithstanding, anecdotal accounts as well as research studies portray boomers as having a long history of needing to be needed and valued. Boomer cohorts focus on possibilities and want to prove their worth to themselves and others. This can be a useful trait to possess, especially if you are planning to continue working.

There is little doubt that boomers will add value and remain active contributors at work, at home, and in their communities. Today, the boomer generation represents 42% of U.S. households and controls 50% of all consumer spending. According to MetLife, to date boomers have the highest median household income in the U.S. and command an estimated spending power of $1.1 trillion. Individuals who turned 60 in 2006 remain substantially satisfied with their lives; at the same time, they are optimistic about an even better future.

Just as when they were young, boomers want to travel, have vacation homes, surround themselves with nice things, and enjoy many comforts of life. Many are managing the demands of being members of a "sandwich generation"—caught between helping elderly parents as well as their grown children. Others are experiencing generativity—a desire to give back to members of the next generation, whether younger workers, grandchildren, or mentees. In mid- and later life, many are reinventing themselves, returning to school, starting businesses, and seeing the world. Most do not want to sit idly by; many have as yet unrealized dreams to pursue. Given their life expectancy, many boomers believe that anything is possible.

You will need to determine how well these descriptions capture your experiences and square off with your individual characteristics. Why and how do you feel the way you do about work, life, and priorities? In addition to your own self-awareness, understanding what shaped the lives of Gen X and Gen Y individuals can provide insights about how you can benefit from their unique talents as well as support their needs. In the following section, you learn more about the attitudes of younger generations to enhance your ability to collaborate with younger generational members and make even more significant contributions in the workplace.

Understanding Generation X

Generation X individuals grew up in the shadow of boomers and were led to believe that they could not match boomers' accomplishments. Born during a time when the birth rate in the U.S. declined, members of this generation were frequently referred to as "baby busters." The term "Generation X" was popularized by a Canadian as a way to describe a nameless generation of individuals who felt that they were overshadowed by the boomers.

Xers are usually thought of as people who were in their twenties during the 1990s; demographers categorize the generation more specifically as individuals born between 1961–1981. According to Strauss and Howe, many younger Gen X members believe that they belong to neither the boomer nor X generation. Others exhibit "generational bilingualism" and define themselves as members of both. Interestingly, shared generational identity emerges when individuals become disillusioned upon entering the labor market or joining the workforce.

Time Magazine referred to Xers as the "twenty-something generation," post-boomers who faced serious issues confronting America. Having witnessed the fall of the Berlin Wall and the end of the Cold War, many Gen X youth saw America strengthen its image as a superpower. In sharp contrast, however, the tide shifted beginning in the 1990s, and individuals experienced the effects of an economic depression. Business downsizing in the U.S. affected friends and families; jobs moved offshore or were outsourced. Traditional employment relationships began to disappear, and young people wondered whether they would be able to find permanence in the workplace or whether their parents would be the last generation to receive Social Security benefits.

The interactions of Gen Xers with teachers, voters, and even their parents contrasted sharply with the indulgences afforded boomers. Piercing their bodies, sporting tattoos, and hiding behind dark glasses, individuals realized that older generations often looked askance at them. The media offered unflattering descriptions and referred to cohorts as slackers—at-risk individuals with rootless ambition. Living in a world of electronic media, eating junk food, watching videos, and worshiping MTV, their behavior conflicted with boomer values as well as with the war on drugs that society was waging. Older adults frequently condemned their music and the unintelligible words emitted from boom boxes. Rap and grunge musical themes of suicide, dying, and homicide further differentiated this generation.

Gen Xers had complex family lives and witnessed a higher rate of parental divorce than any other generation in America. Many children were born outside of marriage or absent a father figure; single parent families and blended families became more and more common. Statistics reported by Strauss and Howe revealed that family configurations varied dramatically with approximately "56% of dependent children living with two, once-married parents, another 14% with at least one previously married parent, 11% with a stepparent, and 19% with one parent." Consequently, the label "latch-key kids" took hold, sending a message that children had to let themselves into the house after school and remain amused until an adult returned from work. Xers quickly learned to be self-directed and personally determined. Gen X characteristics, such as resourcefulness, independence, and self-reliance, were born from youthful experiences that resulted in individuals having few expectations of others. While there were different subgroups or Gen X subcultures, collectively Xers shared a common sense of alienation. Instead of putting their trust in others, they learned to put faith in themselves and carved out an identity of their own.

In addition to issues in their home lives, Xers frequently lacked optimism about the future and had reason to be skeptical about leaders and politics. An energy crisis, AIDS, hostage-taking, gang killings, homelessness, and federal deficits were all serious social problems that loomed large. People also confronted misplaced hero worship as they monitored the downfall of flawed role models such as Nixon, Clinton, and O.J. Simpson. In turn, many young Xers questioned whom to trust. They were indifferent to religion and skeptical that churches, synagogues, or organizations steeped in tradition had anything to offer. Rules often seemed useless as the generation splintered and continued to develop on its own as an alienated youth culture. While some generational members experienced cycles of poverty, dependency, and crime, others found another path.

Technology changed the lives of Gen Xers dramatically. With Walkmans, PCs, VCRs, video games, PDAs, faxes, and cell phones, the infusion of technological innovations was vastly different for Xers in comparison to boomers' experiences with television. Technology was omnipresent. Many Xers became self-taught computer geeks who not only learned about computers, but also through them. The Internet provided instant exposure to the world and awareness of issues of the day, further reinforcing their skepticism. Today, both in the workplace and at home, Xers are proficient at multitasking and experimenting with new and emerging technologies. Most like visuals, images, and pictorials, oftentimes forgetting that many boomers prefer face-to-face or oral communications to computer-based interaction. Based on their own prowess with technology, Xers frequently view boomers as technophobes who are not on board with the latest advances.

Xers' employment history has been volatile with many experiencing difficulties in the job market. Early in their careers, some took temporary or part-time jobs as clerks, cashiers, and service workers despite the fact that they were educated for higher-level work. Although underemployed, financial need was their motive for working. Rather than looking for long-term commitments or promises from employers, many tested their competence as entrepreneurs and took risks that previous generations were unwilling to assume. Some were successful; others were not. Hence a select group of Xers became "boomerangers"—individuals who returned to their parents' homes after unsuccessful bids to achieve success and independence.

Despite cool attitudes, criticism from previous generations, and seemingly detached behavior, streetwise Xers used their know-how to get ahead. Young Xers worked hard and left their problems behind when at work. While many perceived themselves ridiculed by the boomer generation, they were judgmental of boomers. This is ironic because many coveted the affluence and perquisites associated with boomer life; many Xers sought to gain social approval and financial independence despite their unconventional ways.

Xers' distrust of institutions and career uncertainties led many to be cautious and skeptical, especially in their relationships with institutions. Generational members tend to be frank about what they want and need. Their approach to the world of work is survivability, predicated on being self-reliant. Career security is based on having a resume that reflects accomplishments and portable skills. Individuals place tremendous value on having access to information they consider relevant to their work. While many boomers are used to being evaluated once or twice a year, Xers value frequent assessment and solicit input so that they can adapt and respond quickly.

If Xers are not developing on the job, receiving ongoing training, or seeing progress, they may change employers in order to build new competencies in other settings. Remarkably, many do so without fear. Unlike boomers, Xers are unlikely to spend years demonstrating organizational loyalty; instead they may well change jobs four or five times early in their careers. Consequently, boomers often characterize Xers as disloyal or unreliable, perceiving them to be self-centered or even fickle.

Despite the fact that all individuals want to be well compensated for the work they do, money is not the major driver for deciding to stay with a company. A poll of 1,200 Gen X employees reported by *Fortune* (Fisher, 2006) found that 77% of Xers said they would quit in a minute if it meant increased intellectual stimulation at a different company. Additional research corroborates Xers' desire to manage their own time; 51% said they would welcome a chance to telecommute, and 61% of Gen X women stated they would leave their current jobs if offered flexible hours elsewhere. What appeals to you as a boomer may have a decidedly different meaning and value for Generation X.

Xers bring a fresh perspective to the workplace. They have a big picture orientation and strong work ethic. Typically, Generation X individuals like working on teams and collaborating with peers to accomplish objectives and achieve business goals. Desirous of building solid relationships, Xers are more likely to connect with a network of friends who care about them and their well being rather than joining organizations.

Shelton and Shelton found that having positive relationships with colleagues, interesting work, and continuous learning opportunities were important elements for Xers in the workplace. In addition, Fisher noted that Xers seek egalitarian work environments and are less interested in recognition, title, prestige, or power. Individuals tend to be somewhat suspicious of hierarchies and want to participate as equals. Thus, rank and seniority mean little to them. Xers want leaders and managers to "walk their talk" and will call individuals on their behaviors when words do not correspond with deeds. Characteristically committed to achieving and maintaining work-life balance, Xers like to have fun. They desire a life beyond their jobs. This may be a reaction to an overcommitment to work common to boomers. While boomers make work a top priority and link sacrifice with success, Xers disconnect the two and seek freedom and discretion to achieve work-life balance.

Some companies are especially expert at responding to the motivational needs and strengths of Generation X. Chemical maker W. L. Gore put in place a "lattice structure" that interconnects different roles and working relationships without using job titles. While such a structure is unusual, the unique configuration has special appeal to Xers because the organizational chart is not hierarchical; leadership and authority are rotated among team leaders. Other companies, such as Whole Foods, operate on the basis of self-managed teams whereby leadership is passed around. At Intuit, employees at all levels are encouraged to contribute to the development of new products. Examples such as these reflect the changing nature of the workplace and the need to build participatory relationships and teamwork, both of which appeal to Gen Xers as well as boomers. Shelton and Shelton provide evidence that turnover rates in companies that strive to motivate individuals from different generations tend have lower turnover than their competitions.

As a boomer, you can play an invaluable role by helping Xers be successful at work. Although they have a high tolerance for change—a characteristic of boomers early on in their careers—many Xers are less seasoned decision-makers who can benefit from the wisdom of knowledgeable colleagues. Below the surface, individuals want stability and need to believe that someone is willing to invest in them. When that is in place, Xers not only perform, collaborate, and display great zeal, but they also tend to stay on the job.

Xers can learn from you, and likewise you can learn from them. Their informal communication style invites interaction. Reverse mentoring is taking hold in many organizations whereby individuals, regardless of their age or position, share their expertise with seasoned professionals needing to develop specific skills or competences. This approach is founded on reciprocal knowledge-sharing whereby mentees, in turn, share their expertise in areas where their mentors need development. For example, a Gen Xer's technological competence can be the ideal complement to a boomer sharing insights about organizational culture and politics. Reciprocity, collaboration, and valuing one another's contributions—behaviors valued across all generations—can form the basis for a meeting of the minds to enhance cross-generational collegial relationships.

Understanding Generation Y

Also known as Millennials and Gen Next, Gen Y individuals continually strive to overcome negative stereotypes and patterns established by Xers even though both generations are proficient with a variety of technologies. The Internet, DVDs, Wii, cell phones, iTunes, iPhones, iPods, Bluetooth, and Blackberries are second nature to many generational members who grew up with technology during the dot-com boom. In fact, Y individuals perceive themselves to be more technologically proficient and cutting-edge than any previous generation.

Born between 1981–1999, Yers were raised by protective parents who wanted to have children. In contrast to the previous generation's focus on birth control and abortion rights, becoming moms and dads, child-rearing, and family values were important. Many Gen Y individuals had the benefit of stay-at-home moms and dads or single parents to guide their development. Shared parenting arrangements offered children thoughtful caretaking in homes that were free of drugs, alcohol, and cigarettes. Parents, schools, and communities also committed to creating wholesome environments for Y youth. Cars sported "Baby on Board" signs, reflecting the importance of protecting children; test tube babies and in-vitro fertilization offered new hope for childless couples; health foods, G-rated movies, and after-school sports and activities further reinforced the commitment to children's well-being. The government reflected a similar ethic of care, regulating safety standards for infant car seats and encouraging the use of bicycle safety helmets. All these examples are visible symbols of how hopeful people were about the potential of this racially and ethnically diverse generation to contribute to society.

Determined to support this generation, schools worked to provide better education. Teachers enhanced their competencies and standardized curricula, educational standards rose, and graduation requirements became more stringent. Strong rules and principles, quality benchmarks, supervision by adults, and affection from extended family members inspired Y offspring to excel. Sales of books, music, and periodicals for children nearly doubled from 1986–1991, and Disney regained preeminence with child-oriented hits such as *The Lion King* and *Little Mermaid*. Later, Gen Y kids grew up along with Harry Potter. As Gen Y matured, music took yet another turn as alternative rap and pop icons became role models.

Gen Y benefited from dramatic changes taking place in society and, as a consequence, their attitudes and beliefs reflect a significant departure from Gen X and boomer behaviors, actions, and trends. Historians cite legislative decisions that affected the entire generation, reminding us of sharp contrasts in the treatment for Gen X versus Gen Y youth. For example, when Medicare changes took effect in 1990 to ensure benefits for all poor children, individuals born prior to 1983 were excluded from coverage. The *New York Times* reported that boomers demanded more of their offspring then they asked of themselves, not wanting their children to do as they did.

Traumatic events such as the Oklahoma City bombing and violent attacks in schools had significant impact on Yers. In a survey of the high school class of 2000, Gen Y children stated that Columbine, a horrific example of youth gone awry, was the number-one event in their lives. This harrowing tragedy led to renewed interest in protecting children and, as a byproduct, reinforced the need for young adults to be more conforming and to ostracize outsiders. Despite harrowing events in their youth, Yers tend to be more optimistic than Xers and also happier, more confident, and more collaborative. Less suspicious of government and organizations than Xers, most Yers are well behaved; many women and men are sports-oriented and have hobbies. Young Gen Yers are achievers who trust their parents, tend to have good grades, and high goals. A study by the Pew Research Center revealed that 81% of 18–29-year-old Yers said getting rich was their generation's first or second most important life goal; additionally, a Gallup survey validated Gen Y's preoccupation with money; 55% of this same age cohort agreed or strongly agreed that they dream about being rich (Jayson, 2007).

Despite characterizations of the generation's focus on money, most Yers look for suitable employers and want meaningful work—not just a paycheck. In the workplace, Gen Y self-promotion often reflects a "me-first" attitude, which many from this generation believe is the only route to success. Feeling entitled, individuals seek opportunities to change things and, as a consequence, have been called the "Me Generation." Similar to their Gen X predecessors, they seek feedback and on-the-job learning, enjoy challenges, and want variation in what they do. Often resistant to hierarchy, individuals like teamwork and flexible environments that encourage collaboration, fun, and opportunities to engage with the latest technologies.

Communicating with Gen Yers who do most of their talking through a variety of alternate technologies can be a challenge. Their preferred approach to communication includes text messaging rather than face-to-face engagement, which is in sharp contrast to boomers' desire to observe body language and exercise discretion as to whether in-person communication is preferable to email. In addition, Xers' interpersonal communication style, which is direct and to the point, can test boomers. Gen Xers tend to cut to the action quickly without mincing words. They do not see this communication pattern as rude but rather simply a way to learn what they need to know or share in an equally rapid manner. To keep pace with our changing world, many major market employers are tapping the facility Gen X and Gen Y individuals have with technology-driven communication by replacing email, once the state-of- art communication tool, with instant messaging. Companies such as IBM send 2.5 million instant messages a day, capitalizing on the speed with which post-baby boomers can support real-time operations through advanced communications networks. Unfortunately, talking with and through machines can lead to misunderstandings. Observations of workplace interaction reveal that communication is an area where Gen X and Gen Y individuals need to slow down and figure out how to accommodate others' communication styles and preferences.

Based on their technological prowess, Yers are emerging as a generation that is extremely proficient at multitasking. They get things done quickly while focusing on results; consequently, their ability to do many things simultaneously is attractive to employers. Futurists suggest that Yers will most likely have at least ten career changes in their lifetimes. This does not seem to faze generational cohorts who disregard traditional notions that you need to do one job before another; instead, many Yers build parallel careers and enjoy the stimulation that accrues from challenges and learning new things.

> *In a tight labor market, making sure scarce Millennials can cover more than one position is a smart strategy. In a contracting company, it's cost-effective to put millennials' multitasking abilities to use rather than hire more employees. Plus, cross-training is a great retention strategy which reduces the expense of turnover.*
>
> —Lancaster and Stillman

An important goal for Gen Y individuals is to be in the spotlight— the center of attention. Fifty-one percent of respondents in a Pew Research Center Poll, one of the most extensive research of this age group, want to be famous. Researchers believe that MTV and reality shows are furthering such goals. YouTube videos and profiles on My Space and Facebook enable individuals to demonstrate their worth, draw attention to their uniqueness, and tout their value to others whom they don't even know. Studies suggest that rather than just getting what Warhol called "15 minutes of fame," Yers sometimes demonstrate narcissistic attitudes. Twenge warns that having inflated egos and being self-absorbed can cause personal problems in the future if individuals are insulted or rejected.

Gen Y individuals tend to respect authority, but they do not do so blindly. They want to see the benefit or rationale for doing something before getting on board. They resist heavy-handed and micro-management. Given their focus on skill development as opposed to career development, it is important to understand what Gen Y individuals need and want to know. Many employers are striving to accommodate their preferences by customizing approaches to meet individuals' development needs. For example, PricewaterhouseCoopers matches its 2,000 partners with 10–12 employees who check in to see how individuals' lives and work are going to ensure that people remain connected to the firm. Managers are given 30 days to respond to employee requests for feedback upon completion of a project. Although this approach developed in response to the desire of Gen X and Gen Y for feedback and evaluation, such responsiveness is equally applicable and meaningful for you as a boomer.

Whether in the classroom or on the job, Yers ask questions and, above all, want to be heard and acknowledged. Their rapid-fire style and desire to consume information often presents challenges to trainers and consultants. Marriott International has developed bite-size "edutainment" whereby employees can download information to their cells, laptops, and iPods, as opposed to employing more traditional, one-size-fits all development approaches. Company training programs are multisensory and responsive to Yers' comfort levels, although often perceived as stimulus overload for boomers.

Relating Across Generations

It is important to be attuned to Gen X and Gen Y needs, desires, and styles just as savvy employers have responded to yours. Generation-specific research offers insight into what really matters to younger generation members. Surveying the attitudes of more than 1,000 Gen X and Gen Y individuals, the Institute for the Future, in collaboration with Deloitte, explored young people's views about a variety of work-life issues. Three-quarters of those surveyed, regardless of gender, age, income, or race and ethnicity, said that job mobility was extremely important. Of greater significance was people's desire for mobility *within* an organization rather than in the broader labor market. This finding helps to debunk the notion that Gen Y individuals are short-termers; instead it suggests that, like boomers, Yers can make longer-term workplace commitments when satisfied and afforded opportunities to move into new areas and fields. Equally interesting are respondents' self-assessments of their skill sets. Deloitte reported that only about half of study participants said they are good at making decisions based on numbers and data or written communication. Additionally, less than half said they are "very good" or "excellent" at public speaking, setting and keeping to a budget, or selling ideas or things; and, fewer than a quarter ranked themselves as being skillful in a second language. These data suggest that Gen Yers, as well as Gen X individuals, lack some of the basic skills that you and your boomer colleagues developed and honed over the years.

At the same time that younger generation workers want and need development, many are already the poster children for honoring diversity. Pew Research Center's data indicate that Gen Y individuals are more tolerant than boomers and believe that immigrants strengthen society. Yers not only help to narrow gender-role gaps, but they also like and seek opportunities to work with different types of people. While wanting autonomy and independence as they learn and grow, many Gen Yers need to become more proficient at learning how to distinguish risk-taking, in general, from calculated risk-taking based on facts and information. The bottom line for many Gen X and Gen Y individuals is that they want to be judged on their own merits and crave positive reinforcement at accelerated rates.

To what extent do you believe that unique generational talents and worldviews should not pit Gen Y against Gen Xers or boomers but instead should be seen as different styles? As a member of the boomer generation, you have an opportunity to effect change and put to use the various things you've learned about generational differences. At the same time, we encourage you to read between the lines and look for the commonalities between your behaviors when you were young and the traits of Gen X and Gen Y individuals. Similarities are an excellent starting point for conversations!

How can you, as a boomer, make sense of generational differences and build effective working relationships in a multigenerational work environment? Sometimes, reconciling your own values, beliefs, and behaviors with those of others is difficult. However, while cognizant of differences in background and experiences among generational members, we encourage you to consider trying the techniques discussed next.

Appreciate Common Qualities

Based on a seven-year study by the Center for Creative Leadership (CCL), which included more than 5,800 multigenerational individuals born between 1926 and 1986, a book by Deal suggests that boomers have fundamental qualities in common with younger generations. These qualities provide common ground upon which you can build cross-generational relationships. When you commend someone for actions reflecting these qualities, you will find them receptive to seeking common ground on other matters. Let people know you value them as important contributors. Study findings suggest that

- Basic **values** are shared in common among the boomer, X, and Y generations. Conflicts that occur are largely about differences in behavior—how individuals display their values through their actions.

- Individuals in all generations want **respect**. Boomers may want younger persons to respect their decisions; younger persons may want respect for their ideas, suggestions, and recommendations.

- All generations feel that **trust** is important and that it must be earned. You need to show that you know what you are talking about (credibility), do what you say you will do (reliability), and keep the other person's interests at heart (sincerity).

- **Loyalty** to an individual or an organization is important but depends on the context. Younger workers may change jobs frequently, but they are still loyal to employers while they are there.

Encourage and Support Continual Learning

Another common quality across the three generations described in this chapter is the view that learning and development is important. Persons of all ages want to acquire new skills and knowledge so that they can perform their current jobs well and progress in their careers. As a boomer, you can act as a mentor, coach, or at least a confidant to Gen X or Y individuals. You can help them develop an understanding of the organizational culture and how to get things done. Of course, you can also share your knowledge and insights on work-related matters. Organizations are increasingly eager to have knowledge passed along from generation to generation.

Provide Open Communications to Set a Climate for Collaboration

CCL's research sought to determine just how significant generational differences really are. Based on study findings, Deal proposed that what most individuals perceive as a generational conflict may simply be a reflection of competition among individuals for influence and control. Wanting influence, power, or authority holds true across generations. Boomers want to maintain their clout, while younger individuals want to increase theirs. Older persons in authority tend to make decisions and expect younger individuals to follow them. However, Gen X and Gen Y individuals are more likely to ask questions, seek clarification about decisions, and expect to know the rationale for doing something. This may cause boomers to feel threatened, unduly challenged, or undermined. To work effectively with others, you need to recognize this potential conflict over power—and the importance of open communications.

If you are the one sharing information and shaping decisions, strive to make your thinking process transparent and the facts clear. In addition, ask for feedback from others so that you know how they are reacting to your approaches and can discover how effectively they think you are communicating and involving them in the decision-making process.

Build Personal Relationships, One-on-One

Working with younger generation workers can be as challenging for boomers as working with you can be for Gen X and Gen Y individuals. Be careful not to assess the merits of individuals based on the similarity of their attitudes and behaviors to your own; accept differences and focus on their strengths and what they accomplish. Build reciprocal relationships that involve genuine give and take rather than hierarchy. Although relating to peers may be easier, frequent talking and working with younger persons leads to informal rapport. You may also try to tailor how you work with people based on their preferences and distinctive qualities. Whether you are a colleague or a boomer manager, you have the potential to create an environment where all ages can flourish.

Adapt Your Own Behaviors to Build Mutual Understanding and Collaboration

Identify actions you can choose to initiate as part of a go-forward plan to break down barriers, real or imagined, to enhance intergenerational collaboration. Adopt alternative behaviors that promote age-friendly work environments and minimize intergenerational conflict. In so doing, assess each situation and do the right thing. As a boomer, you have a choice about how to engage across generations as you search for common ground. Important similarities exist among all generations that can form the basis for developing trusting and productive relationships with others. In the workplace, ask yourself these questions:

- To what extent am I frustrated with someone because he or she isn't doing what I think is correct or isn't acting how I would behave?
- Are the dynamics of my interaction with Gen X or Gen Y individuals based on a tug-of-war about who will gain supremacy or who has the most power or authority?
- How do I now view others in light of what I've learned about their history and what may have shaped the behaviors I am experiencing?

- What can I do to seek clarity about the real cause of conflicts rather than automatically attributing the problem to generational differences?

- What actions can I take proactively to open a dialogue, defuse conflict, modify my own behaviors, or, ideally, eliminate the source of the problem?

Manage an Age-Diverse Workforce

As a savvy boomer manager, you have an opportunity to take the lead to ensure a constructive blend of talent and transform workplace practices in response to generational diversity. Strive to find a balance between reliance on traditional management practices and more collaborative, flexible, and creative ones. While managers and employers have become aware of the need to take generational differences into account, the key to successful cross-generational relationships is reciprocity. You can benefit from what younger generation individuals have to offer just as they can benefit from you. Make time to care about what others think, figure out how you can help instead of hinder, and view differences as opportunities for you to stretch and grow as both a leader and colleague. Remember the adage, "Diversity is the one true thing we all have in common." Celebrate it every day.

References

The following are sources utilized by the authors in writing this book. You are encouraged to dig deeper into topics of interest to you. Many of these publications report the results of research studies that support statements made in this book and provide additional information that you may find informative and useful.

Introduction

AARP (1999). *Baby Boomers Envision Their Retirement: An AARP Segmentation Analysis*. Washington, D.C.: AARP.

Dennis, H. (December 12, 2006). Podcast interview. http://wsj.com.

Drucker, P. (2001). *Management Challenges for the 21st Century*. New York: HarperCollins.

Frank, T. (2005). *What's the Matter with Kansas? How Conservatives Won the Heart of America*. New York: Owl Books.

Gross, J. (December 30, 2006). "Elder-care costs deplete savings of a generation." http://www.nytimes.com.

Lancaster, L.C. and Stillman, D. (2002). *When Generations Collide: Who They Are. Why They Clash*. New York: Harper Collins.

Merrill Lynch (2002). *The New Retirement Survey*. New York: Merrill Lynch.

MetLife (2006). *Living Longer, Working Longer: The Changing Landscape of the Aging Workforce—a MetLife Study*. New York: MetLife Mature Market Institute.

Munnell, A.H., Buessing, M., Soto, M., and Sass, S. (July 2006). *Will We Have to Work Forever?* Boston: Center for Retirement Research at Boston College, Issue in Brief, Series 4.

Munnell, A.H. (2006). *Policies to Promote Labor Force Participation of Older People.* Boston: Center for Retirement Research at Boston College.

Prensky, M. (2001). *Digital Game-Based Learning.* New York: McGraw Hill.

Strauss, W. and Howe, N. (1991). *Generations: The History of America's Future, 1584–2069.* New York: William Morrow.

Walker, J. and Lazer, H. (1978). *The End of Mandatory Retirement.* New York: Wiley.

Watson Wyatt (2004). *Compensation and Benefit Strategies to Retain Older Workers.* New York: Watson Wyatt.

Chapter 1

Ahern, A. (2007). *Snap Out of It Now.* Sentient Publications.

Butler, T. (2007). *Getting Unstuck: How Dead Ends Become New Paths.* Boston: Harvard Business School Press.

Campbell, J. (1949). *Hero with a Thousand Faces.* Princeton University Press.

Crandell, S. (2007). *Thinking About Tomorrow.* New York: Warner Wellness.

Dychtwald, M. (2003). *Cycles: How We Will Live, Work, and Buy.* New York: The Free Press.

Gladwell, M. (2007). *Blink: The Power of Thinking Without Thinking.* New York: Little, Brown.

Goffee, R. and Jones, G. (December 2005). "Managing Authenticity." *Harvard Business Review,* pp. 87–94.

Holt, J. (January 21, 2007). "You are what you expect: the futures of optimists and pessimists." *New York Times Magazine*, pp. 12–13.

Levinson, D. (1986). *The Seasons of a Man's Life*. New York: Ballantine Books.

Remen, R.N. (1997). *Kitchen Table Wisdom: Stories that Heal*. New York: Riverhead Trade.

Ruffenach, G. (May 13, 2007). "What couples don't talk about: retiring." (http://online.wsj.com/article/SB117900578530001141.html).

Sedlar, J. and Miners, R. (2003). *Don't Retire, REWIRE*. Indianapolis, IN: Alpha Books.

Seligman, M. (2002). *Authentic Happiness: Using the New Positive Psychology to Realize Your Potential for Lasting Fulfillment*. New York: Free Press.

Sheehy, G. (1976). *Passages: Predictable Crises of Adult Life*. New York: E.P. Dutton.

Sheehy, G. (1995). *New Passages*. New York: Ballantine.

Welch, J. (2001). *Jack: Straight from the Gut*. New York: Grand Central Publishing.

Chapter 2

AARP and Towers Perrin (2005). *The Business Case for Workers Age 50+: Planning for Tomorrow's Talent Needs in Today's Competitive Environment*. Washington, D.C.: AARP.

Atchley, R. (1989). "A continuity theory of aging." *Gerontologist*, pp. 29, 183–190.

Calvo, E. (2006). *Does Working Longer Make People Healthier and Happier?* Boston: Boston College Center for Retirement Research at Boston College.

Dychtwald, K. and Kadlec, D. (2005). *The Power Years*. New York: Wiley.

Erikson, E. (1950). *Childhood and Society*. New York: Norton.

Feldman, D.C. (1994). "The decision to retire early: A review and conceptualization." *Academy of Management Review*. pp. 10, 285–311.

Feldman, D.C. and Kim, S. (2000). "Bridge employment during retirement: A field study of individual and organizational experiences with post retirement employment." *Human Resource Planning*. pp. 23, 30–35.

Greene, K. (September 26, 2005). "When we're all 64." *Wall Street Journal*. pp. R1.

Hunt, D., Ramji, S., and Walker, P. (2005). "Taking the risk out of retirement." *The McKinsey Quarterly*, No. 2, pp. 72–91.

Merrill Lynch (2005). *The New Retirement Survey*. New York: Merrill Lynch.

MetLife (2006). *Living Longer, Working Longer: The Changing Landscape of the Aging Workforce—A MetLife Study*. MetLife Mature Market Institute.

Special Committee on Aging, U.S. Senate (2005). *Living Stronger, Earning Longer: Redefining Retirement in the 21st Century Workplace*. Washington, D.C.: U.S. Government Printing Office (Serial No. 109-6).

Towers Perrin (2003). *Back to the Future: Redefining Retirement in the 21st Century*. Stamford, CT: Towers Perrin.

Watson Wyatt (2004). *Phased Retirement: Aligning Employer Programs with Worker Preferences*. New York: Watson Wyatt Worldwide.

Watson Wyatt (2004). *Compensation and Benefit Strategies to Retain Older Workers*. New York: Watson Wyatt.

Zissimopoulos, J. and Karoly, L. (2007). *Work and Well-Being Among the Self-Employed at Older Ages*. Washington, D.C.: AARP Public Policy Institute.

Chapter 3

AARP (2006). *In Their Dreams: What Will Boomers Inherit?* Washington, D.C.: AARP.

AARP (2006a). *Boomer Wealth—Beware of the Median.* Washington, D.C.: AARP. Data Digest #143.

Bernstein, A. (June 5, 2006). "When boomers cash out." *Business Week.*

Carlson, R.C. (2004). *The New Rules of Retirement: Strategies for a Secure Future.* New York: John Wiley & Sons.

Chatzky, J. (September 21, 2006). "Just when you thought it was safe to retire." *CNNMoney.com.*

Cullen, T. (October 12, 2006). "Fiscally fit: A policy to live by." *Wall Street Journal.*

Deloitte (2005). Annual 401(k) Benchmarking Survey. New York: Deloitte.

Duhigg, C. (July 8, 2007). "For elderly investors, instant experts abound." *New York Times,* pp. 1, 14.

Eisenberg, L. (2006). *The Number: A Completely Different Way to Think About The Rest of Your Life.* New York: Free Press.

Federal Reserve Board (March 22, 2006). "Recent changes in U.S. family finances: evidence from the 2001 and 2004 Survey of Consumer Finances." *Federal Reserve Bulletin,* A1–37.

Greene, K. (July 29, 2006). "Will my medical benefits still be there in retirement?" *Wall Street Journal,* pp. B4.

Kennickell, A.B. (2003). *A Rolling Tide: Changes in the Distribution of Wealth in the U.S.,* Table 10. Annandale-on-Hudson, NY: Bard College, Levy Economics Institute.

Lim, P. J. (August 20, 2006). "Take my nest egg, please." *New York Times.*

Lowenstein, R. (October 30, 2003). "The end of pensions?" *New York Times*.

Machan, D. (September 12, 2006). "Stay rich." SmartMoney.com.

Merrill Lynch (2004). *Retirement: The American Dream*. New York: Merrill Lynch.

Merrill Lynch (2005). *The New Retirement Survey*. New York: Merrill Lynch.

Munnell, A.H., Buessing, M., Soto, M., and Sass, S. (July 2006). *Will We Have to Work Forever?* Center for Retirement Research at Boston College, Issue in brief, Series 4.

National Association of Insurance Commissioners (2003). *A Shopper's Guide to Long-Term Care Insurance*. Kansas City, MO: NAIC. http://www.naic.org.

Novelli, W.D. (May 2006). "The future of pensions." *AARP Bulletin*.

Opdyke, J.D. (November 4, 2006). "New Rx for long-term care." *Wall Street Journal*, pp. B1.

PBS (2006). "Interview: Jack VanDerhei." www.pbs.org/wgbh/pages/frontline/retirement/interviews/vanderhei.html.

Porterfield, B. (September 25, 2006). "Retiree health care could be a back-breaker." *San Diego Union Tribune*, pp. 1.

Powell, E.A. (December 10, 2006). "Boomers' retirement boom." *San Diego Union-Tribune*, pp. H3.

Rix, S.E. (2004). *Aging and Work—A View from the United States*. Washington, D.C.: AARP.

Spectrem Group (2007). *Affluent Market Report*. www.spectrem.com.

Towers Perrin (2003). *Back to the Future: Redefining Retirement in the 21st Century*. Stamford, CT: Towers Perrin.

U.S. Trust (2006). *What the Wealthy Think: The U.S Trust Annual Survey of Affluent Americans*. http://www.ustrust.com.

Vernon, S. (2004). *Live Long and Prosper*. New York: Wiley.

Ware, C. (2006). *Rightsizing Your Life*. New York: Springboard Press.

Watson Wyatt (May 3, 2006). *New Analysis Shows Largest U.S. Companies Continued Shift to 401(k) Plans in 2005*. Arlington, VA: Watson Wyatt. Press Release.

Watson Wyatt (2006). *Retiree Health Benefits: Time to Resuscitate?* Arlington, VA: Watson Wyatt.

Chapter 4

AARP and Towers Perrin (2005). *The Business Case for Workers Age 50+: Planning for Tomorrow's Talent Needs in Today's Competitive Environment*. Washington, D.C.: AARP.

Arnst, C. (March 11, 1998). "The new era of lifestyle drugs." *Business Week*.

Auster, B.B. (April 24, 2004). "The fountain of youth." *U.S. News and World Report*.

Avolio, B.J., Waldman, D.A., and McDaniel, M.A. (1990). "Age and work performance in nonmanagerial jobs: The effects of experience and occupation type." *Academy of Management Journal*, 32, pp. 407–422.

Barrick, M.R., Mount, M.K., and Judge, T.A. (2001). "Personality and performance at the beginning of the new millennium: What do we know and where do we go next?" *International Journal of Selection and Assessment*, 9, pp. 9–30.

Bee, H.L. (1996). *Journey of Adulthood* (3rd ed). Englewood Cliffs, NJ: Prentice Hall.

Begley, S. (November 16, 2006). "How to keep your aging brain fit: Aerobics." *Wall Street Journal*.

Berger, K.S. (1990). *The Developing Person Through the Life Span* (4th ed). New York: Worth Publishers.

Bertrand, A. (February 11, 2007). "Time to debunk those fitness myths." *Albany Democrat Herald*.

Bielby, B. and Bielby, D. (2000). "Hollywood dreams, harsh realities: Writing for film and television." Contexts. *American Sociological Review*, Fall/Winter.

Birren, J.E. (1964). *The Psychology of Aging*. Englewood Cliffs, NJ: Prentice Hall.

Birren, J.E. (1974). "Translations in gerontology—from lab to life: Psychophysiology and speed of response." *American Psychologist*, 29, pp. 805–815.

Bishof, L.J. (1969). *Adult Psychology* (2nd ed). New York: Harper & Row.

Botwinick, J. (1967). *Cognitive Processes in Maturity and Old Age*. New York: Springer.

Botwinick, J. (1970). "Geropsychology." In P.H. Mussen and M.R. Rosenzweig (Eds). *Annual Review of Psychology*. Palo Alto, CA: Annual Reviews.

Botwinick, J. (1973). *Aging and Behavior: A Comprehensive Integration of Research Findings*. New York: Springer.

Bromley, D.B. (1966). *The Psychology of Human Aging*. Baltimore, MD: Penguin.

Butler, R.N. (1975). *Why Survive? Being Old in America*. New York: Harper & Row.

Calvo, E. (2006). *Does Working Longer Make People Healthier and Happier?* Boston: Boston College Center for Retirement Research.

Cattell, R.B. (1963). "Theory of fluid and crystallized intelligence: A critical experiment." *Journal of Educational Psychology*, 54, pp. 1–22.

Cattell, R.B. (1987). *Intelligence: Its Structure, Growth, and Action.* Amsterdam: North-Holland.

Chudacoff, H.P. (1989). *How Old Are You? Age Consciousness in American Culture.* Princeton, NJ: Princeton University Press.

Cohen, G.D. (2000). *The Creative Age: Awakening Human Potential in the Second Half of Life.* New York: Avon Books.

Cross, K.P. (1981). *Adults as Learners: Increasing Participation and Facilitating Learning.* San Francisco: Jossey-Bass.

Crowley, C. and Lodge, H.S. (2004). *Younger Next Year: A Guide to Living Like 50 Until You're 80 and Beyond.* New York: Workman Publishing.

Davidson, K. (September 18, 2006). "Entrepreneur backs research on anti-aging." *San Francisco Chronicle*, pp. B1.

deGrey, A. and Rae, M. (2007). *Ending Aging: The Rejuvenation Breakthroughs that Could Reverse Human Aging in our Lifetime.* New York: St. Martin's Press.

Donlon, M.M., Ashman, O., and Levy, B.R. (2005). "Revision of older television characters: A stereotype-awareness intervention." *Journal of Social Issues.* 61, pp. 2, 307.

Dooren, J.C. (February 7, 2007). "Dementia tied to loneliness in the elderly." *Wall Street Journal.* Health Section D4.

Dressel, P. (1988). "Gender, race, and class: Beyond the feminization of poverty in later life." *The Gerontologist.* 28 (8), pp. 177–180.

Fogel, R.W. (2005). *Changes in the Disparities of Chronic Disease in the Course of the 20th Century.* National Bureau of Economic Research. NBER Working Paper #10311.

Forrester Research Inc. (2003). *The Wide Range of Abilities and Its Impact on Computer Technology.* Cambridge, MA.

Friedan, B. (1993). *The Fountain of Age*. New York: Touchstone.

Gardner, H. (1983). *Frames of Mind*. New York: Basic Books.

Gardner, H. (1995). "Reflections on Multiple Intelligence: Myths and Messages." *Phi Delta Kappan*, 77(3), 200–209.

Gergen, M. and Gergen K. (1994). *Social Construction: A Reader*. Thousand Oaks: Sage Publications.

Goleman, D. (1995). *Emotional Intelligence: Why It Can Matter More Than IQ*. New York: Bantam Books.

Green, R.F. (1972). "Age, intelligence, and learning." *Industrial Gerontologist*, 2, pp. 29–40.

Gullette, M.M. (1997). *Declining to Decline*. Charlottesville: University of Virginia Press.

Harlson, D. and Parker, S. (January 21, 2003). "Age and job searching." *USA Today*.

Harvard Health Publications (February 8, 2007). *Healthbeat: Eat Healthy for Life*. Boston, MA: Harvard Medical School.

Hedge, J.W., Borman, W.C., and Lammlein, S.E. (2005). *The Aging Workforce: Realities, Myths, and Implications*. Mountain View, CA: Mayfield Publishing.

Horn, J.L. (1976). "Human abilities: A review of research theory in the early 1970s." In M.R. Rosenzwieg and L.W. Porter (Eds). *Annual Review of Psychology*, 27, pp. 437–485.

Horn, J.L. (1982). "The theory of fluid and crystallized intelligence in relation to concepts of cognitive psychology and aging in adulthood." In F.I.M. Craik and Trehub (Eds). *Aging and Cognitive Processes*. pp. 238–278. New York: Plenum.

Horn, J.L. (1985). "Remodeling old models of intelligence." In B.B. Wolman (Ed). *Handbook of Intelligence: Theories, Measurements, and Applications*. NY: Wiley.

Horn, J.L. and Donaldson, G. (1976). "On the myth of intellectual decline in adulthood." *American Psychologist*, 31, pp. 701–719.

Horn, J.L. and Donaldson, G. (1980). "Cognitive development in adulthood." In O.G. Brim and J. Kagan (Eds). *Constancy and Change in Human Development*. Cambridge, MA: Harvard University Press.

Hoyer, W.J. and Touron, D.R. (2003). "Learning in adulthood." In J. Demick and C. Andreoletti (Eds). *Handbook of Adult Development*. pp. 23–41. New York: Kluwer Academic/Plenum Publishers.

International Longevity Center—USA (2006). *Ageism in America: The Status Reports*. New York: International Longevity Center-USA, Ltd.

Knox, A. (1977). *Adult Development and Learning*. San Francisco: Jossey-Bass Publishers.

Kolata, G. (July 30, 2006). "So big and healthy grandpa wouldn't even know you." *New York Times*.

Kolata, G. (July 28, 2006). "We're living longer, healthier than ever." *Arizona Daily Star*.

Lohman, D.F. and Scheurman, G. (1992). "Fluid abilities and epistemic thinking: Some prescriptions for adult education." In A. Tuijnman and M. van der Kamp (Eds). *Learning Across the Lifespan: Theories, Research, Policies*. Oxford: Pergamon Press.

Merriam, S. and Caffarella, R. (1999). *Learning in Adulthood: A Comprehensive Guide* (2nd ed). San Francisco: Jossey-Bass.

Merrill, S.S. and Verbrugge, L.M. (1999). "Health and disease in midlife." In S.L. Willis and J.D. Reid (Eds). *Life in the Middle: Psychological and Social Development in Middle Age*. San Diego, CA: Academic Press.

Moody, H. (2002). *Aging: Concepts and Controversies* (4th ed). Thousand Oaks, CA: Sage Publications.

MyPrimeTime. http://www.myprimetime.com.

National Institute on Aging (March 2006). "The Future of Human Life Expectancy: Have we reached the ceiling or is the sky the limit?" *Research Highlights in the Demography and Economics of Aging*. Bethesda, MD: National Institute on Aging.

Perls, T. and Silver, M. (2000). *Living to 100: Lessons in Living to Your Maximum Potential at Any Age*. New York: Basic Books.

Polmore, E. (1970). *Normal Aging*. Durham, NC: Duke University Press.

Prairie Public Television (2005). "A guide to health aging: A healthworks special." Retrieved 12-12-05 from http://www.prairiepublic.org.

Rees, J.N. and Botwinick, J. (1971). "Detection and decision factors in auditory behavior of the elderly." *Journal of Gerontology*, 26, pp. 133–136.

Rix, S. (2002). *Update on the Older Worker*. Washington, D.C.: AARP Research Center.

Roisen, M.F. and Oz, M.C. (2007). *You: Staying Young—The Owner's Manual for Extending Your Warranty*. New York: Free Press.

Rowe, J.W. and Kahn, R.L. (1998). *Successful Aging*. New York: Pantheon Books.

Sadler, W.A. (2000). *The Third Age: Six Principles for Growth and Renewal After Forty*. Cambridge, MA: Perseus Publishing.

Schaie, K.W. (1983)."The Seattle longitudinal study: A 21-year exploration of psychometric intelligence in adulthood." In K.W. Schaie (Ed). *Longitudinal Studies of Adult Psychological Development*. pp. 64–135. New York: Guilford Press.

Schaie, K.W. (1994). "The course of adult intellectual development." *American Psychologist*. 49(4), pp. 303–313.

Schaie, K.W. (1996). "The course of intellectual development in adulthood." In J.E. Birren and K.W. Schaie (Eds). *Handbook of the Psychology of Aging* (4th ed). Orlando, FL: Academic Press.

Schaie, K.W. (1996). *Intellectual Development in Adulthood: The Seattle Longitudinal Study*. Cambridge: University of Cambridge Press.

Schaie, K.W. (1974). "Translations in gerontology—from lab to life: Intellectual functioning." *American Psychologist*, 29, pp. 802–807.

Schaie, K.W. and Willis, S.L. (1983). *Adult Development and Aging* (2nd ed). Boston: Little Brown, 1986.

Selye, H. (1956). *The Stress of Life*. New York: McGraw-Hill.

Simonton, D.K. (1998). "Career paths and creative lives: A theoretical perspective on late life potential." In Carolyn El Adams-Price (Ed). *Creativity and Successful Aging: Theoretical and Empirical Approaches*. pp. 3–18. New York: Springer.

Sternberg, R.J. (1985). *Beyond IQ: A Triarchic Theory of Human Intelligence*. Cambridge: Cambridge University Press.

Sternberg, R.J. (1996). *Successful Intelligence: How Practical and Creative Intelligence Determine Success in Life*. New York: Simon & Schuster.

Sterns, H.L. and Kaplan, J. (2003). "Work, leisure, and retirement." In J. C. Cavenaugh and S.K. Witbourne (Ed). *Gerontology: An Interdisciplinary Perspective*, pp. 235–390. New York: Oxford University Press.

Taeuber, C. (1990). "Diversity: The Dramatic Reality." In Scott A. Bass, Elizabeth A. Kutza, and Fernando (Eds). In *Diversity and Aging*, pp. 1–45. Glenview, IL: Scott Foresman.

Thorndike, E.L., Bregman, E.O., Tilton, J.W., and Woodyard, E. (1928). *Adult Learning*. New York: McMillan.

Vaillant, G.E. (2002). *Aging Well: Surprising Guideposts to a Happier Life from the Landmark Harvard Study of Adult Development.* Boston: Little, Brown, and Co.

Willis, S.L. and Schaie, K.W. (1994). "Cognitive training in the normal elderly." In F. Forette, Y. Christensen, and F. Boller (Eds). *Cerebral Plasticity and Cognitive Stimulation.* Paris: Foundation Nationale de Gerontologie.

Chapter 5

Brown, K. (2003). *Staying Ahead of the Curve.* Washington, D.C.: AARP.

Cohen, G. (2000). *The Creative Age.* New York: Avon Books.

Corbett, D. and Higgins, R. (2007). *Portfolio Life.* San Francisco: Jossey-Bass.

Drucker, P. (2001). *Management Challenges for the 21st Century.* New York: HarperCollins.

Duka, W. and Nicholson, T. (December 2002). "Retirees Rocking Old Roles." AARP Bulletin.

Frankl, V. (2004). *Man's Search for Meaning.* New York: Random House

Freedman, M. (1999). *Prime Time: How Baby Boomers Will Revolutionize Retirement and Transform America.* Cambridge, MA: Public Affairs.

Freedman, M. (2007). *Encore.* Public Affairs.

Handy, C. (1998). *The Age of Unreason.* Boston: Harvard Business School Press.

Hewlett, S.A. and Luce, C.B. (November-December, 2006). "Extreme jobs: The dangerous allure of the 70-hour workweek." *Harvard Business Review.*

Hibbert, G. (1936). *Studies in Quaker Thought and Practice, Part II.* London: Friends' Home Service.

Kanter, R.M. (2006). "Back to college." *AARP Magazine,* July/August.

Kellaway, L. (May 29, 2006). "Don't blame extreme jobs for a predicable loss of libido." *Financial Times.*

Lawler, E. (2003). *Treat People Right: How Organizations and Individuals Can Propel Each Other into a Virtuous Spiral of Success.* San Francisco: Jossey-Bass.

Leider, R. (1997). *The Power of Purpose: Creating Meaning in Your Life and Work.* San Francisco: Barrett-Koehler.

McCrudden, C., Bourne, A, and Lyons, C. (2005). *You Unlimited.* London: Management Books 2000 Ltd.

MetLife Foundation and Civic Ventures (2005). *New Face of Work Survey: Documenting the Desire to Work in the Second Half of Life.* Princeton Survey Research International.

Nash, L. and Stevenson, H. (2004). *Just Enough: Tools for Creating Success in Your Work and Life.* Wiley.

Pope, E. (April 10, 2007). "Reinvention: Charting a career's turning point." *New York Times.*

Portfolio Life. http://www.globalideasbank.org.

Ramey, V. and Francis, N. (2007). *A Century of Work and Leisure.* San Diego: University of California at San Diego.

Terez, T. (2002). *22 Keys to Creating a Meaningful Workplace.* Adams Media Corporation.

Wilson, L. (2006). *Civic Engagement and the Baby Boomer Generation.* Haworth Press.

Chapter 6

Aslanian, C.B. (2001). *Adult Students Today*. New York: College Board.

Aslanian, C.B. and Brickell, H.M. (1980). *Americans in Transition: Life Changes As Reasons for Adult Learning*. New York: College Entrance Examination Board.

Atchely, R.C. (1976). *The Sociology of Retirement*. Cambridge, MA: Schenkman.

Bardwick, J. (1995). *Danger in the Comfort Zone*. New York: Amacom.

Bee, H.L. and Bjorkland, B.R. (2004). *The Journey of Adulthood* (3rd ed). Englewood Cliffs, NJ: Prentice Hall.

Christianson, S.L., Palkovitz, R. (1998). "Exploring Erikson's psychosocial theory of development: Generativity and its relationship to parental identity, intimacy, and involvement with others." *Journal of Men's Studies*, 7, pp. 133–156.

Csikszentmaihalyi, M. (1996). *Creativity: Flow and the Psychology of Discovery and Invention*. New York: Harper Collins.

Creighton, S. and Hudson, L. (2002). *Participation Trends and Patterns in Adult Education: 1991 to 1999*. Washington, D.C.: National Center for Educational Statistics, Office of Educational Research and Improvement, U.S. Department of Education.

Cross, K.P. (1982). *Adults as Learners*. San Francisco: Jossey-Bass.

Deal, J. (2007). *Retiring the Generation Gap: How Employees Young and Old Can Find Common Ground*. San Francisco: Jossey-Bass.

Ekerdt, D. J., Bosse, R., and Levkoff, S. (1985). "Empirical test for phases of retirement: Findings from the normative aging study." *Journal of Gerontology*, 49, pp. 95–101.

Ekerdt, D.J., Kosloski, K., and DeViney, S. (2000). "The normative anticipation of retirement by older adults." *Research on Aging*, 22, pp. 3–22.

Elderhostel (January 2005). *What Will Baby Boomers Want from Educational Travel?* Boston, MA: Elderhostel, Inc.

Ellin, A. (November 11, 2006). "No more knitting. Older students want enlightenment." *New York Times.*

Erikson, E.H. (1963). *Childhood and Society* (2nd ed). New York: Norton.

Gall, T.L., Evans, D.R., and Howard, J. (1997). "The retirement adjustment process. Changes in the well-being of male retirees across time." *Journal of Gerontology: Psychological Sciences*, 52, pp. 110–117.

Hansson, R.O., DeKoekloek, P.D., Neece, W.M., and Patterson, D.W. (1997). "Successful aging at work. The older worker and transitions to retirement." *Journal of Vocational Behavior*, 51, pp. 202–233.

Havighurst, R.J. (1972). *Developmental Tasks and Education* (3rd ed). New York: McKay.

Houle, C.O. (1961). *The Inquiring Mind*. Madison: University of Wisconsin Press.

Houle, C.O. (1988). *The Inquiring Mind* (2nd ed). Madison, WI: University of Wisconsin Press and Norman Oklahoma Research Center for Continuing and Professional Higher Education.

Kim, K., Collins Hagedorn, M., Williamson, J., and Chapman, C. (2004). *Participation in Adult Education and Lifelong Learning: 2000–2001*. U.S. Department of Education.

Kleinginna, P.Jr. and Kleinginna, A. (1981). "A categorized list of emotion definitions, with suggestions for a consensual definition." *Motivation and Emotion*, 5, pp. 345–379.

Lancaster, L.C. and Stillman, D. (2002). *When Generations Collide*. New York: Harper Collins Publishers.

Levinson, D.J., Darrow, C.N., Klein, E.B., Levinson, M.H., and Mc-Kee, B. (1978). *Seasons in a Man's Life*. New York: Knopf.

Levinson, D.J. and Levinson, J.D. (1996). *Seasons in a Woman's Life*. New York: Ballantine.

MetLife Foundation and Civic Ventures (2005). *New Face of Work Survey: Documenting the Desire to Work in the Second Half of Life*. Princeton Survey Research International.

Morstain, B.R. and Smart, J.C. "Reasons for participation in adult education courses: A multivariate analysis of group differences." *Adult Education*, 24(2) pp. 83–98.

Neugartern, B. (1979). "Time, age, and the life cycle." *American Journal of Psychiatry*, 136, pp. 887–893.

Palmore, E.B., Burchett, B.M., Fillenbaum, G.G., George, L.K., and Wallman, L.M. (1985). *Retirement: Causes and Consequences*. New York: Springer.

Pasupathi, M., Staudinger, U.M., and Baltes, P.B. (2001). "Seeds of wisdom: Adolescents' knowledge and judgment about difficult life problems." *Developmental Psychology*, 37, pp. 351–361.

Sheehy, G. (1996). *New Passages: Mapping Your Life Across Time*. New York: G. Meritt Group.

Sheehy, G. (1976). *Passages: Predictable Crises of Adult Life*. New York: Bantam.

Simonton, D.K. (1990). "Does creativity decline in later years: Definition and theory." In Marion Permutter (Ed). *Late Life Potential*. Washington, D.C.: Gerontological Society of America, pp. 83–112.

Szinovacz, M. and Ekerdt, D.J. (1995). Families and retirement in R. Blieszner and V. H. Beford (Eds). *Handbook of Aging and the Family*. Westport, CT: Greenwood.

Trani, E.P. (2001). *Lifelong Learning*. June presentation, Virginia Commonwealth University.

Tough, A. (1971). *The Adult's Learning Projects*. Toronto: Ontario. The Ontario Institute for Studies in Education.

Vaillant, G.E. (2002). *Aging Well*. Boston: Little Brown.

Chapter 7

Aaronson, S., Fallick, B., Figura, A., Pingle, J., and Wascher, W. (Spring, 2006). "The recent decline in the labor force participation rate and its implications for potential labor supply." *Brookings Papers on Economic Activity*, vol. 1, pp. 69–134.

Anderson, P. "Digital dauphins: Youth vs. age in tech." (http://archives.cnn.com/2001/CAREER/trends/01/30/agebias/index.html).

Associated Press (2006). "Ageism in America." http://www.msnbc.msn.com/id/5868712.

Bernanke, B.S. (February 28, 2007). *Long-Term Fiscal Challenges and the Economy*. Federal Reserve Board, Presentation to the House of Representatives.

Bolles, R. (1972). *What Color Is Your Parachute?* Berkeley, CA: Ten Speed Press.

Bureau of Labor Statistics (2004). Employment Projections through 2014. www.bls.gov.

Cappelli, P. (2003). "Will there really be a labor shortage?" *Organizational Dynamics*, Vol., 32, No. 3, pp. 221–233.

Conference Board (2005). *Managing the Mature Work Force*. New York: The Conference Board.

Delong, D.W. (2004). *Lost Knowledge: Confronting the Threat of an Aging Workforce*. New York: Oxford University Press.

Ernst & Young (2006). *The Aging of the U.S. Workforce: Employer Challenges and Responses*. New York: Ernst & Young.

Frauenheim, E. (October 9, 2006). "Face of the Future: The Aging Workforce." *Workforce Management*. pp. 1, 22–26.

Freeman, R.B. (2006). *Is a Great Labor Shortage Coming? Replacement Demand in the Global Economy*. Cambridge, MA: National Bureau of Economic Research. http://www.nber.org/papers/w12541.

General Accounting Office (2001). *Older Workers: Demographic Trends Pose Challenges for Employers and Employees*. Washington, D.C.: GAO-02-85.

Government Accountability Office (2006). *Baby Boom Generation: Retirement of Baby Boomers Is Unlikely to Precipitate Dramatic Decline in Market Returns, But Broader Risks Threaten Retirement Security*. Washington, D.C.: GAO-06-718.

ILC-USA Anti-Ageism Task Force (2006). *Ageism in America*. International Longevity Center, http://www.ilcusa.org.

Judy, R., D'Amico, C., and Geipel, G. (1997). *Workforce 2020*. New York: Hudson Institute.

Kaihla, P. (September 1, 2003). "The coming job boom." *Business 2.0 Magazine*.

Knowledge@Wharton (May 17, 2006). *The Immigration Debate: Its Impact on Workers, Wages, and Employers*. http://knowledge.wharton.upenn.edu.

Leonard, B. "Aging baby boomers bring age bias to the forefront." http://www.shrm.org/hrnews_published/archives/CMS_012572.asp.

Miller, F. and Katz, J. (May 2004). *The Boomer Bust—Big Problems Ahead for Organizations*. Link and Learn Newsletter, www.link-ageinc.com.

Myers, D. (2007). *Immigrants and Boomers: Forging a New Social Contract for the Future of America*. New York: Russell Sage Foundation.

Reynolds, S., Ridley N., and Van Horn, C. (Summer, 2005). "A Work-Filled Retirement: Workers' Changing Views on Employment and Leisure." *WORKTRENDS Survey*, Vol. 8.1.

Skladany, R. and Sumser, J. (2006). "Boomers to Bust Age Bias? Baby Boomers Redefine Retirement—Ageism Is the Next Frontier." http://www.retirementjobs.com.

Su, B.W. (November 2005). "The U.S. economy to 2014." *Monthly Labor Review*, Vol. 128, No. 11, pp. 10–24.

Toossi, M. (November 2005). "Labor force projections to 2014: retiring boomers." *Monthly Labor Review*, Vol. 128, No. 11, pp. 25–44.

Toossi, M. (2006). "A new look at long-term labor force projections to 2050." *Monthly Labor Review*, Vol. 129, pp. 19–39.

Twenge, J.M. (2006). *Generation Me: Why Today's Young Americans Are More Confident, Assertive, Entitled—and More Miserable Than Ever Before*. New York: Free Press.

Walker, J. and Merryman, A. (2005). *Workforce Architecture: Aligning Talent with Strategy Through Segmentation*. La Jolla: HR Strategic Issues Council.

Wall Street Journal Online (2006). "Go Figure—Careers." http://online.wsj.com/article/infogrfx_go_figure_careers.html.

Weintraub, D. (February 18, 2006). "Boomers will soon see benefits of immigrants." *Sacramento Bee*.

Chapter 8

AARP (2006). *Boomers Turning 60*. Washington, D.C.: AARP.

Campbell, K. (January 26, 2005). "The many faces of the baby boomers." *Christian Science Monitor*.

Chao, L. (2005). "For gen exers, it's work to live: Finding the right job/life balance." *Wall Street Journal Online*. http://www.careerjournal.com, retrieved 3/20/06.

Chester, E. (2002). *Employing Generation Why? Understanding, Managing, and Motivating Your New Workforce*. Lakewood, Colorado: Tucker House Books.

Coupland, D. (1991). *Generation X: Tales for an Accelerated Culture*. New York: St. Martin's Griffin.

Deloitte Development LLC (2005). *Connecting Across the Generations in the Workplace: What Business Leaders Need to Know to Benefit from Generational Differences*.

Deloitte Development LLC (2006). *Flexibility and Choice: What Business Leaders Need to Know to Connect Across Generations in the Workplace*.

Fisher, A. (January 20, 2006). "What do gen xers want?" *Fortune Magazine*.

Gordon, L. and Sahagun, L. (February 27, 2007). "Gen y's ego trip takes a bad turn." *Los Angeles Times*.

Heffernan, Virginia (March 28, 2007). "Apart from wanting it all, what makes boomers so special?" *New York Times*. pp. B9. http://www.nyt.com.

Hicks, R. and Hicks, K. (1999). *Boomers, Xers, and Other Strangers*. Wheaton, Illinois: Tyndale House Publishers.

Holsti, O.R. and Roseau, J.N. (1980). "Does where you stand depend on when you were born? The impact of generation on post-Vietnam policy belief." *The Public Opinion Quarterly*, 44, pp. 1–22.

Howe, N. and Strauss, W. (2000). *Millennials Rising: The Next Great Generation*. New York: Vintage Books.

Hughes, M.E. and O'Rand, A.M. (2004). *The Lives and Times of Baby Boomers*. Russell Sage Foundation and Population Reference Bureau. http://www.prb.org accessed 3-8-07.

Institute for the Future (2004). *The Future Workforce: Young People's Views on Careers, Employers, and Work*. San Francisco, CA.

Jayson, S. (January 10, 2007). "The Goal: Wealth and Fame." *USA Today*.

Jones, Landon Y. (1980.) *Great Expectations: America and the Baby Boom Generation*. New York: Coward, McCann & Geoghegan,

Karp, H., Fuller, C., and Sarias, D. (2002). *Bridging the Boomer Xer Gap. Creating Authentic Teams for High Performance at Work*. Palo Alto, CA: Davies-Black Publishing.

Krepcio, K. (December 4, 2006). *Baby Boomers in Retirement: Implications for the Workforce*. Keynote Remarks, Inaugural Forum and Dedication of the Ronald I. Coun Center for Creative Maturity.

Lancaster, L. and Stillman, D. (2002). *When Generations Collide*. New York: Harper Collins.

Manneheim, K. (1952). *Essays on the Sociology of Knowledge*. New York: Columbia University.

Martin, C.A. and Tulgan, B. (2006). *Managing the Generation Mix: From Urgency to Opportunity*. Amherst, MA: HRD Press.

Maslow, A. (1943). "A theory of human motivation." *Psychological Review*. 50, pp. 370–396.

Massey, M. (1970). *The People Puzzle: Understanding Yourself and Others*. Reston, Virginia: Reston Publishing.

Massey, Morris (2006). *What You Are Is Where You Were When . . .Again*. Video. Cambridge, MA: Enterprise Media.

MetLife Mature Market Institute (2005). *A Profile of American Baby Boomers*. New York: MetLife.

National Commission on Excellence in Education (1983). *A Nation at Risk: The Imperative for Educational Reform*. Washington, D.C.: U.S. Department of Education.

Neuman, S. (1965). *Permanent Revolution: Totalitarianism in the Age of International Civil War* (2nd ed). London: Pall Mall Press.

New York Times. (November 30, 1995). "The 60s generation, once high on drugs, warns its children."

Raines, C. (1997). *Beyond Generation X: A Practical Guide for Managers*. Menlo Park, CA: Crisp Publications.

Roper Starch Worldwide (1999). *Baby Boomers Envision Their Retirement: An AARP Segmentation Analysis*. Roper Starch Worldwide Inc. and AARP.

Sachs, D. (2006). *Scenes from the Culture Clash*. Fast Company. January/February. pp. 73–77.

Schuman, H. and Rieger, C. (1992). *Generations and Collective Memories*. American Sociological Review, 54, pp. 359–381.

Shelton, C. and Shelton, L. (2005). *The neXt Revolution: What Women Want at Work and How Their Boomer Bosses Can Help Them Get It*. Mountain View, CA: Davies-Black Publishing.

Society for Human Resources Management (2004). *Generational Differences Survey Report*, pp. 1–29.

Strauss, W. and Howe, N. (1999). *Generations: The History of America's Future, 1584 to 2069*. New York: William Morrow.

Strom, D. (April 5, 2006). "IM generation is changing the way business talks." *New York Times*.

Tulgan, B. (1997). *The Manager's Pocket Guide to Generation X*. Amherst, MA: HRD Press.

Tulgan, B. (2000). *Managing Generation X: How to Bring Out the Best in Young Talent*. New York: Norton.

Thau, R.D. and Heflin, J.S. (1997). *Generations Apart: Xers vs. Boomers vs. the Elderly*. New York: Prometheus Books.

Zemke, R., Raines, C., and Filipczak, B. (2000). *Generations at Work: Managing the Clash of Veterans, Boomers, Xers, and Nexters in Your Workplace*. New York: American Management Association.

Wall Street Journal. (January 29, 1990). "Boomers: The 'not as I did' parents."

INDEX

Symbols

401(k), 54-56

A

AARP, 29
accentuating strengths, 74-75
access to desired opportunities,
  factors to consider during
  decision-making, 20-21
activities, meaningful activities,
  91-92
  choosing, 102-105
  community or charitable
    activities, 96-99
  leisure activities, 94-95
  personal learning and growth,
    99-100
  professional work, 92-94
  social interaction, 95-96
Adam@home comic strip, 82
adopting learning mindsets,
  127-128
affirmation, 95
age discrimination, 147
  challenging, 151-152
age ranges of those in workforce,
  137-138

age-diverse workforces,
  managing, 181
ageism, 73
aging
  decline in capabilities, 65-69
    *capacity to learn and solve
      problems, 71-72*
    hearing, 69
    intelligence, 68
    memory, 71
    reaction time, 70
    vision, 69
  functional age, 75-76
Anderson, P., 151
annuities, sources of income,
  58-59
appearance, dealing with
  stereotypes, 76-77
applying what you learn, 130
assessing your situation, asking
  the right questions, 3-4
auditory learning, 123
Avenue Montaigne, 14
avoiding smoking, 81-82

W Wharton School Publishing

In the face of accelerating turbulence and change, business leaders and policy makers need new ways of thinking to sustain performance and growth.

Wharton School Publishing offers a trusted source for stimulating ideas from thought leaders who provide new mental models to address changes in strategy, management, and finance. We seek out authors from diverse disciplines with a profound understanding of change and its implications. We offer books and tools that help executives respond to the challenge of change.

Every book and management tool we publish meets quality standards set by The Wharton School of the University of Pennsylvania. Each title is reviewed by the Wharton School Publishing Editorial Board before being given Wharton's seal of approval. This ensures that Wharton publications are timely, relevant, important, conceptually sound or empirically based, and implementable.

To fit our readers' learning preferences, Wharton publications are available in multiple formats, including books, audio, and electronic.

To find out more about our books and management tools, visit us at whartonsp.com and Wharton's executive education site, exceed.wharton.upenn.edu.

Wharton
UNIVERSITY of PENNSYLVANIA

Pearson
Education